D1306851

CAN'T MISS™

container
GARDENING

Practical Solutions for Gardening Success

Published by Cool Springs Press, a Division of Thomas Nelson, Inc., P.O. Box 141000, Nashville, Tennessee 37214.

Cataloging in Publication Data is available.
ISBN: 1-5918-6156-X

First printing 2005
Printed in the United States of America
10 9 8 7 6 5 4 3 2 1

Managing Editor: Cindy Kershner
Copyeditor: Sara J. Henry
Cover Design: Becky Brawner, Unlikely Suburban Design
Book Design: Bruce Gore
Production Artist: S.E. Anderson
Cover Photo: Charles Mann

Cool Springs Press books may be purchased in bulk for educational, business, fundraising, or sales promotional use. For information, please email SpecialMarkets@ThomasNelson.com.

Visit the Thomas Nelson website at **www.ThomasNelson.com** and the Cool Springs Press website at **www.coolspringspress.net**.

CAN'T MISS™

container
GARDENING

Practical Solutions
for Gardening
Success

Felder Rushing
& Teri Dunn

COOL SPRINGS PRESS
A Division of Thomas Nelson Publishers
Since 1798

acknowledgements

I wish it were possible for me to personally thank the now-anonymous woman gardener who, when I was seven years old, gave me a rooted plant in a pot (it was a *Sansevieria*), that died but spurred me on to learn why and what to do next time. And I especially want to acknowledge the furiously-paced work of Cindy Kershner, who, working with the Cool Springs Press editorial staff, pulled this book together and helped Teri and me become a fun writing team!

—Felder Rushing

Thanks to Cindy Kershner; to Jenny Andrews, Ramona Wilkes, and Hank McBride; to David Lindley and Wally Ingram . . . *y los tres amigos.*

—Teri Dunn

contents

Color Your World with
Container Plants

g ardeners and potted plants have been "growing" a rich, practical tradition together for thousands of years, a tradition that continues today. Container-grown herbs, vegetables, fruits, and flowers have gotten people through hard times, and uplifted their spirits.

Egyptian temple carvings dating back to 1495 BC picture frankincense trees in pots. The ruins of Pompeii include many courtyard garden pots, which were space- and water-conservative in an otherwise hot, dry, crowded city. And Chinese wall paintings in tombs dating back to the Tang Dynasty depict miniature or "bonsai" trees in pots.

Just to cheer up his wife, Nebuchadnezzar II (604-562 BC), who lived in what is now known as Iraq, is credited for building the legendary Hanging Gardens of Babylon—one of the Seven Wonders of the ancient world—watered from the Euphrates River far below.

Potted coffee and palm trees were brought from the New World by early explorers, in spite of requiring precious drinking water needed by thirsty sailors; special containers were built to conserve moisture and protect plants from salty ocean air. Gardeners for Louis XIV at Versailles were supplied with nearly two million clay pots for growing the bedding plants needed to continuously change out the extensive flower garden beds to please the Sun King—sometimes as often as two or even three times a day!

Before the 1940s, when plastic pots and soilless potting soils were made widely available, most people used whatever they could find to grow plants—often wooden boxes and flour or whiskey barrels cut in half. Today's greenhouse industry uses hundreds of millions of plastic pots every year for growing plants in greenhouses and fields and transporting them to garden centers and landscape sites. The sheer numbers of those pots is fueling a modern recycling and reusing program.

Why Container Gardening?

Regardless of what they are made of—clay, plastic, wood, metal, leather, or any other nonporous material—containers for growing plants can be tall or wide, large

Container gardening's popularity jumped 45 percent between 1998 to 2003 with gardeners spending more than $1 billion on pots and container plants.

Growing plants in containers dates back to ancient times.

WARDIAN CASES AND THE ORANGERIE AT VERSAILLES

The wooden planters in this photograph are similar to the ones used in Versailles centuries ago.

One famous ancestor of our sun rooms and side porches wrapped with clear plastic for overwintering potted plants was at Versailles, the fabulous country palace of French king Louis XIV, built in the late 1600s. It included more than one thousand fruit trees, many of them citrus, growing in large formal wooden boxes. To keep them from freezing in the winter, King Louis had a cathedral-like room built into a south-facing wall beneath one of his famously intricate parterre flower gardens, into which the tender trees could be brought in October and held until the following spring.

To keep the trees warm, the large openings of the room were covered with movable glass panes that allowed sunlight (solar energy) to stream in, yet trapped most of the heat (radiant energy) inside, much like a closed car on a sunny winter day. This orangerie at Versailles still works perfectly well.

But even though gardeners have temporarily covered up tender plants with bell-shaped glass jars since at least 500 BC, it wasn't until 1827 that small, portable greenhouses were invented—by accident. Dr. Nathaniel Ward, an English physician, noticed that ferns were growing quite well inside enclosed glass cases in spite of cold weather and London's severe air pollution. His "Wardian cases" are now known as terrariums.

These totally enclosed plant containers revolutionized the way we grow plants in harsh conditions. By reducing the dramatic changes in climate and rapid swings in day and night temperatures during long sailing voyages, they made possible the importation of sensitive plants from all over the world. This altered how Europeans and Americans alike gardened.

Cold frames, used by gardeners to keep plants warm in cold weather, are large Wardian boxes.

or small, or heavy or light enough to hang. In general, they have to be sturdy enough to hold soil and the roots of plants without tipping over, yet be portable enough to arrange and rearrange artistically and be moved around to take advantage of—or escape—changing weather. They can be brought indoors during extreme weather. Most have drainage holes in the bottom to allow excess water to drain out.

Pots enable us to grow tropical plants far away from the tropics, and herbs up close where we can better enjoy and harvest them. They can line walks, can be grouped for mass effect, or can be placed as accents. They can be strictly practical conveniences, or add form and color to the landscape.

A Growing Hobby

Container gardening's popularity jumped 45 percent between 1998 to 2003, according to the National Gardening Association, with gardeners spending more than $1 billion on pots and container plants. And there are reasons for this.

Blue is always a favorite color for containers. It sets off both flowers and foliage.

As we continue to live in ever-crowded cities, our balconies and patios are becoming important "outdoor rooms" from which we can escape the TV and supper dishes. Containers of beautiful flowers, sculptural trees, and herbs and vegetables give us another contact with the natural world.

Potted plants even improve the air we breathe; researchers seeking ways to make it practical to travel in space and live under the sea have demonstrated how potted plants capture and filter out airborne pollutants from our home and office environments. Self-watering planters are designed with built-in water reservoirs that create a continuous "capillary" or wicking action to keep soils moist for weeks at a time, without overwatering.

Finally, container gardens are more sensible for an aging society that is finding the digging and stooping of conventional gardening less desirable. Container gardening can only increase in popularity and practicality—beginning, of course, in our own home gardens.

Where Does Your Garden Grow?

With very few exceptions, the plants in this book can be grown in containers anywhere in the country—from Key West to San Diego, Boston to Seattle,

RAISED BEDS, ROCK GARDENS, AND BERMS

Sometimes a regular container is not large enough or needs watering too often. Three basic kinds of oversized, "modified dirt piles" can be created, and are used like oversized container gardens. Other than portability, there is very little difference in how plants are grown in these built-up areas and large pots.

There's a history to this. When Captain John Smith began his little English colony at Jamestown, the settlers quickly found that their vegetables and herbs needed extra drainage in the wet winters, so they built up the native soil with more soil and organic matter, creating long, triple-wide permanent garden rows outlined with wooden boards. These "raised beds" drained well, warmed up quickly in the spring, and made working the soil, planting, and harvesting much easier.

Modern raised beds are merely large, low, bottomless containers, often shored up with wood, brick, stone, or other materials. They can be built up high enough that people with back pain or problems reaching can still enjoy their gardens.

Rock gardens are simply high raised beds of very well-drained sandy soil, lined with rocks and boulders, and usually planted with cacti, succulents, dwarf conifers, and other alpine (mountain) plants that require quickly-draining soils.

A low artificial hill with gently sloping sides, called a "berm" by landscapers, may not look like a container, but it is valuable for helping large plants get the extra drainage they need to grow in otherwise low or wet areas. Berms are usually edged with erosion-resistant groundcovers, turf, or mulch.

This large brick planter is planted and treated like a small raised bed.

and even Anchorage. However, some plants grow best where the nights are cool, while others are much easier to grow and more productive over a longer period in warmer parts of the country.

For all areas except the sub-tropical counties of southern California and the southern half of Florida, you must be prepared to bring in or cover tender potted plants. Many container gardeners replace heat-tolerant summer annuals in the fall with more cold-hardy winter flowers. And quite a few perennials, vines, bulbs, and even woody shrubs can be left out all winter in the frigid northern areas of our continent.

Learn the average first and last frost dates for your area, and meet either your county Extension Service agent and Master Gardeners, or a dependable garden center employee, for highly localized advice. And check the individual plant listings in Chapter 5 of this book for special growing tips or needs.

So when you begin growing plants in containers—from choosing the best pots and selecting plants, through learning about designing with them, and, finally, caring for them—you will find it very easy, and you will have fun.

And in the end, if for any reason something doesn't work out, you can simply empty the pot, select new plants, and keep going. What could be easier?

You can place containers in your garden, and they'll add to the show. Move them later during the season, or change out the planting.

NOW OR LATER

Most container garden experts recommend starting out with small plants spaced far enough apart to allow room for them to grow and fill in to become the size you expect. This is very sensible advice. However, some of us like to cram stuff in so it looks great immediately; we just don't want to wait. This often leads to crowding, increased water and fertilizer needs, and diseases caused by poor air circulation. We end up having to prune or even remove entire plants. But it sure looks good early on!

What Makes a Perfect Plant Container

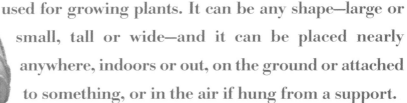

thousands of different kinds of plants can be grown in containers—some better than others. But what makes a great container? Plain and simple: Anything natural, man-made, or recycled that can hold a little soil without tipping over can be used for growing plants. It can be any shape—large or small, tall or wide—and it can be placed nearly anywhere, indoors or out, on the ground or attached to something, or in the air if hung from a support.

There are many materials, styles, and kinds of pots, each with its own unique combination of qualities, advantages, and drawbacks. A container of some type or another can be bought, made, or found to fit every garden situation. Containers make it possible to grow flower, foliage, or edible plants where it would seem nothing would normally be found growing.

Entire gardens can be grown in large bottomless containers called raised beds, which can themselves be made of a variety of materials. Water gardens are containers of sorts, as are the terrariums used for growing humidity-loving plants indoors.

Your choice of container can make or break how a plant grows in it and how the plant and container duo looks, including how the combination blends into or contrasts with the rest of your landscape. It can contrast or complement the plants growing in it, or be used as an accent itself in the garden or home (large pots or urns are often used as design elements, even without plants in them!). A container can be purely functional, decorative, or totally hidden.

There are also various accessories you can use with your plants, from saucers for catching drainage water, to "pot feet" for raising plants above the ground, floor, or deck for better air circulation.

With this huge array of great container possibilities, what makes a container great? How many styles are there? What should it be made of? How can it best be used? This chapter deals entirely with the basics of containers themselves, how they work, and how they can work for you and your plants.

A container may simply be the vessel that holds the plants, or sometimes it can be a work of art.

Elements of a Good Container

There are two considerations for choosing a container for plants: The material of which it is made, and how it is shaped or constructed for good plant growth.

Without trying to be too obvious, a container should be made of a material that is not toxic to plant roots and doesn't dry out too quickly or overheat in the sun, as that can kill plant roots. A very dark pot (for example, the black plastic pots that most garden center plants come in) may need to be shaded by other plants or set inside another pot to keep direct sunshine off it.

To last a long time, the container should be made of a durable material that won't melt or fall apart after repeated watering, or crack if left outside

Containers Should Be:

- nontoxic to plant roots and won't overheat in the sun
- the right size for the plants you want to grow
- made of durable material that resists the effect of water, sun, and cold

- the right porosity for your watering habits or plant roots' need for oxygen
- heavy enough to not fall over
- well drained with a hole in the bottom

Materials:

- Plastic is inexpensive and versatile, but may not breathe well.
- Terra-cotta is unglazed pottery, usually inexpensive, but it but wicks and cracks.
- Glazed pottery is durable, but can crack.
- Wood is rustic and easy to work with for special containers, but will rot.

- Concrete is very durable and cold resistant, but is heavy and comes in few forms.
- Metal is creative and versatile, and usually long lasting.
- Hanging baskets can be plastic, or metal frames lined with moss or fiber.

in freezing weather. Some types of plastic pots will get thin and brittle if exposed to the sun for many months.

The porosity of a pot—its resistance or ability to allow air and water to move through it—can affect how fast a plant dries out, how often it needs watering, and even whether or not enough oxygen can get to roots.

A pot should be the right size for the plant or plants you want to grow in it. If it is too small, plant roots will be constricted and the potting soil will dry out more quickly, so watering will have to be done more often—which washes fertilizers out more quickly. If it is too small or lightweight, the pot will sooner or later fall over under the weight of the plant, especially in strong, gusty winds. If the pot is too large for its plants, it can hold water too long and lead to root rot.

Unless you are growing water plants, a pot must have at least one hole in the bottom to let excess water drain out; otherwise, roots will simply rot, or potting soil will develop a rotten smell. The hole can be covered with screen or broken pottery to keep soil from washing out.

Even if you have no yard, you can still have a garden. Pots of *Sedum acre*, viola, ivy, petunias, geraniums, and more welcome visitors to this house.

Materials for Containers

Some gardeners insist that one kind of pot is better than another, but this is not true. All

ADDING A DRAINAGE HOLE

Put a hole in the bottom of a solid pot by using a special masonry drill bit, or by turning the pot upside down and using a small nail held very close to, but not actually touching, the center of the bottom. Use a hammer to lightly tap the nail so it barely pecks the bottom of the pot to chip away a little at a time until a hole is formed. Be very careful to not hold the nail directly against the pot, or hit the nail too hard, or the pot will crack.

of them have pros and cons, beginning with what they are made of. You can either choose a material that suits your gardening needs or style, or adapt your gardening techniques (especially watering) to accommodate a different material.

The most common materials used for containers are plastic or clay, but wood, metal, concrete, treated paper products, and other materials can easily be used as well, as long as they conform to the basic elements of what makes a pot good (size, drainage hole, and so on).

Over time, terra-cotta pots will crack and break if left outside.

Plastic

Pots made of plastic or other synthetic polymer material can be molded into many shapes and sizes, and are generally lightweight, durable, and inexpensive, although some cheap ones break down in the sunshine and thick, ornate ones may be fairly expensive. Even small plastic trash bins can be used for containers, as long as they have drainage holes cut into the bottoms.

Nonporous plastic pots do not "breathe," which can cause problems for plants whose roots need extra drainage or oxygen. You can reduce or get around these potential problems simply by varying your potting soil ingredients and your watering techniques.

Terra-cotta or Unglazed Clay

Though most gardeners are familiar with red clay pottery, there are many different kinds of clay, with different qualities and densities. The thickness and density of the pot and the temperature at which it was

"fired" or baked influence how quickly the material will absorb water—to "wick" dry in the sun, to allow dissolved fertilizers to pass through, or to crack and flake during winter freezes.

Terra-cotta pots come in many sizes and styles, including traditional or standard ones that are slightly taller than they are wide, or "azalea" pots that are shorter and wider. All types come

If the wind blows a clay pot over, it will likely break. There are plastic pots that look like terra-cotta, but they are weather-resistant and lightweight.

POT MAINTENANCE

Protect Your Pots. Protect expensive glazed pots, and extend the useful life of unglazed and wood containers, by planting in slightly smaller plastic pots and slipping them into the prettier pots.

Repairing Pottery. Broken pottery can be cleaned, dried, and glued back together with epoxy glue. Mix the two components—one part glue, one part hardener—before you cement the pieces, and apply the mix to both parts before joining them. Wipe off spilled glue or use sandpaper to remove dried residue. Use tape to hold the pieces together until they completely harden.

If repairing doesn't work, cracked pots can be used to cover holes in the bottom of other pots or recycled as filler material in the bottoms of larger pots. They and their saucers can also be used to line flower beds, or broken into tiny bits and worked into the edge of a flower bed to deter moles, voles, and digging cats or dogs.

Check Clay Pots for Cracks. Whether terra-cotta or glazed, clay pots are easily cracked or chipped. To check a clay pot for cracks that may be too small to see, simply pick it up, holding it upright from the bottom, and lightly tap its rim with your fingernail. An uncracked pot rings like a bell when tapped; a cracked pot makes a "thunk" sound. If pots in a stack get stuck together, don't force them apart; lightly tap and wiggle all the way around to loosen the tight spot.

with or without a thicker rim, which is not only decorative, but gives more strength and helps provide a grip when pots need to be moved.

Very inexpensive "Mexican" pottery is usually grainy and very porous and baked at low temperatures. Because it often "melts" after prolonged exposure to water or the outdoors elements, it is considered more ornamental than durable. You can treat the insides with a lacquer to help prolong its service life.

Clay that has had extra ingredients added to the surface and is fired at very high temperatures have a slick surface that is impenetrable to water. These pots are often very colorful and sometimes patterned, and last much longer than unglazed terra-cotta.

CAN'T MISS TIP:

PROLONG THE LIFE OF WOOD CONTAINERS

Help prolong the life of wooden containers by sanding, smoothing, and preparing the surface, cleaning with wood deck cleaners; and using wood preservatives or exterior-grade paints and stains. Using plastic liners only partially helps because drainage holes must be cut in the bottom, and moisture gets between the plastic and wood sides.

Wood

Because it can't be formed or cast like plastic or clay, wood is less versatile; it has to be cut and then nailed, screwed, or glued. Wood can easily be used for making large square tubs, long narrow window boxes, or raised beds. It can also be custom-made into nearly any size by home gardeners or contractors to fit special sites, and can be painted easily to complement a home's architecture.

Containers made of wood—including the very

Wood containers can be beautiful, especially when they're filled with spring-blooming bulbs.

Clay pots usually develop a crusty white coating on the outside. This is simply the dissolved fertilizer (called "salts") and water additives that are left as water evaporates from the outside of the pots. This rarely poses a problem to plants and can be easily gotten rid of. Simply water the plants well, wait until the outside of the pots get moist and the salts get slightly dissolved again, then use a plastic brush or dish scrubber to scour it off.

Green algae on the outside of pots—which some gardeners actually prefer, along with dissolved salt buildup, for its "antique" look—is the result of lots of water, lots of fertilizer, and lots of humidity. Treat it the same as you would a salt buildup, and try using less fertilizer on your plants.

If you suspect some plants in a pot died from root disease and want to disinfect pots between uses, soak them in a mild chlorine bleach and water solution for a few hours, then scrub the inside and outside with a stiff plastic or natural bristle brush.

popular half whiskey barrels and bushel baskets, which are usually lined with plastic—generally don't last very long because they rot after prolonged contact with soil and moisture. Even treated wood will decay after awhile. New "fake" wood, made from a blend of recycled plastic and sawdust, is very easy to work with and very long lasting.

Concrete

Most places that sell outdoor pottery also offer large concrete containers that can be painted to suit the gardener. Though very heavy, and not all that inexpensive, concrete is extremely durable and very resistant to cold in the winter. It can be cast into square, rectangular, or round forms and is often found with fairly ornate trimming or other design. Concrete cinder

The weight and roughness of these weathered troughs and urns contrasts with the delicate *Campanula, Helianthemum,* and *Dianthus.*

Be creative in the garden with containers. Here, drainage tiles have been stair-stepped and planted with grasses and succulents—a good way to add plants that need perfect drainage.

Pots set right on the ground, patio, deck, or floor, often have trouble draining because the drainage hole is easily stopped up. And the constantly seeping water and dissolved fertilizers on wood decks or floors will absolutely leave a stain, or even rot the wood. Two easy ways of dealing with this are using saucers to catch extra water, or using "pot feet"—small objects, usually three or four, placed under the pots—to raise them up for better drainage and air circulation.

Saucers, which look best if they are matched with their pots in both material and in size, should be deep enough to catch and hold a fair amount of water without overflowing. Terra-cotta saucers absorb water that usually evaporates quickly if the saucers are also raised up above the deck or floor; otherwise they can leave stains on a deck or floor.

Saucers are also important indoors for helping provide humidity for tropical plants. By placing several small containers of tropical plants on top of gravel in a large saucer, humidity is dramatically increased.

If you don't soak up the excess water in a saucer, it can keep potting soils from draining, which can rot roots. It is a good idea to keep a large "bulb baster" handy to suck up excess water from a saucer before it overflows.

Pot feet are simply small gadgets used to lift pots and saucers a little ways off the ground. It takes at least three to do the job. They allow for air circulation underneath, help with excess water evaporation, prevent stains and spots on floors and deck, and can even help reduce the number of "critters" (worms, snails, ants, roly-polys) from getting into pots. By using pot feet to raise containers above the water level in trays or large saucers, even ants cannot get to the pots themselves.

Ornamental pot feet are sold wherever pottery is sold, but homemade ones can be fashioned from small rocks, bits of brick, pieces of wood, or even crushed aluminum cans.

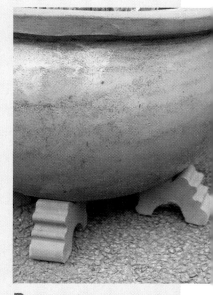

Pot feet are decorative and allow water to drain away from the container. The roots of many plants will rot if left sitting in water over a period of time.

Even vines can grow in containers, as these clematis growing in lead containers demonstrate.

blocks used for building walls can easily be used for small planters, especially in informal settings. They can be painted just like wood.

A special blend of concrete and basic potting soil ingredients can be formed into a lighter, homemade material called "hypertufa" (see chapter 4 for instructions on how to make a hypertufa pot).

Metal

Metal containers are very trendy, and can be stamped into interesting shapes with designs. Tin, aluminum, copper, iron, and other metals are used, and many gardeners save old cooking pots, large tin cans that food came in, and other recycled metal containers for growing plants. Many upscale gardeners use antique or replicas of Victorian urns made of cast iron.

Hanging baskets made from wire require a lining of sphagnum moss or fiber mat. Special rust-proofing paints are available to slow or eliminate rust, which weakens metal.

Other Materials

Virtually anything that has the elements of a good container can be used—including cut-open bags of potting soil, used car tires, and chimney flue tiles. However, these creative materials usually give a strong impression, and can easily be overdone and run the risk of clashing with plants and the overall theme of a garden.

When choosing other materials for containers, be sure they meet the basic requirements of what makes a container good.

CAN'T MISS TIP:

SPARE YOUR BACK

Moving large containers that are not already on rolling platforms can be a real backbreaker. Try tipping the containers (with help) and putting an old carpet, rug, or blanket underneath so you can drag them. For very large containers, use a dolly or hand truck, borrowed or rented for a fraction of what one might cost. To move large pots up steps, make a ramp with two sturdy boards and a rope for secure leverage.

Styles of Containers

Containers come in many shapes and styles, for different effects. The large wood tubs at Versailles in France are classic containers that were used to grow large plants and small trees that had to be moved indoors during the winter. Concrete or cast iron urns have been molded after the classic designs of several centuries ago. Brightly colored glazed pottery from Asia can add a zesty, contemporary look to a garden. And no real cottage garden would seem right without a mismatched hodgepodge of various recycled containers.

The most familiar pots are called standards and are taller than they are wide, and larger at the top than the bottom. Plastic ones can be smooth or ribbed (ribbed helps roots develop better, with less likelihood of "girdling" roots going round and round); clay pots usually have the number of inches in diameter on the bottom.

Azalea or fern pots are wider than tall, and are well suited for fibrous-rooted plants, annuals, and bulbs. Because of their lower center of gravity, they are ideal for plants that are likely to blow over during windy weather.

Bulb pots are usually not much more than deep saucers, because bulbs have very shallow roots and need very little soil, but they can also be used

No real cottage garden would seem right without a mismatched hodgepodge of various recycled containers.

One idea can have very different effects when used on different containers. Both containers have plants that mimic hair, but the results certainly vary!

Use your imagination when you think of what to use as containers. The bed, chair, and shoes seem to tell a story, in addition to holding a pretty collection of spring flowers.

Consider a plant container as an investment—both for your pocketbook and for the plant that will have to live in it twenty-four hours a day, seven days a week. Its style and material may have a huge impact on how visitors view your garden.

Regardless of the style, material, and size, consider how long the container will likely last in your garden. You may want something cheap and temporary for flowers or vegetables for just one season of the year, or something you expect will have to be moved quite often (apartment to apartment, or even indoors or out with the seasons). Some gardeners choose very special containers for long-term ownership, as valued heirlooms to pass down through several generations.

Keep in mind that a large pot with several plants in it is easier to care for than several smaller pots that must be moved around or watered a lot. And it is better to start with the pot just big enough to grow your plants and repot into the next size larger as needed, than to put small plants in a big pot and risk overwatering them.

In general, the thicker and heavier, the more durable a container will be and the longer it will last. If the pot will be kept outside all year, it should be of the most durable material possible. If it will be moved a lot, consider a "coaster" with wheels on the bottoms.

for shallow-rooted annuals such as lettuces and for succulent plants. Bonsai pots are also usually very shallow compared with their width.

Tall, tapered Spanish pots are interesting, and raise plants high enough to enjoy up close. However, they are difficult to water correctly, and mostly are used for tap-rooted plants and stylistic effect with the addition of sticks or other decorative non-plant materials.

Other interesting containers include half-baskets for hanging on walls, stackable containers, self-watering containers, "chair" pots (made by replacing the seats with fabric filled with potting soil and plants), raised beds, terrariums, and rooftop gardens. Each has unique characteristics that make it useful in situations where more mainstream containers are less suited.

The Choice Is Yours

Choosing great plants for your garden is one thing, but the type of containers you plant them in can make or break the effect and ease of growth. There are many dozens of possible styles, sizes, shapes, and materials from which to choose, so take your time and find the perfect pot for your perfect plants.

In this example, leftover construction material becomes a series of planters and a fountain.

This chicken container planted with violas makes a pretty display.

What Container Plants Need to Succeed

When growing plants in pots, the most important thing you need to be aware of is that this is not a "normal" life for a plant. Most of our favorite flowers, foliage plants, fruits, and vegetables are from different parts of the world, and naturally grow in different conditions.

Plants growing in containers have special needs that you as a gardener should be prepared to provide. Because the growth of potted plants is tightly restricted—especially their roots—they can't forage for what they need, making them almost totally dependent on you to provide for those needs.

Your understanding of the basics of what plants need for long, productive lives is the first step toward having success with them in your home or garden. But simply knowing what to do doesn't get the job done: Caring for potted plants is a never-ceasing responsibility, and without care the plants will grow poorly, decline, or even die.

This doesn't have to be difficult to understand or do. You really don't need to know a lot about the science—soil pH, microclimates, light lumens, cation exchange capacity, and the like—to have a great container garden. Just remember that, in general, plants grown in containers have the same basic needs as those grown in the ground. Though many different kinds of plants are grown in pots, each has a fairly predictable range of growing requirements, including both environmental and cultural needs.

Pest control can be a real headache with container plants. Some plants are very susceptible to insect or disease problems, and should be left to the most experienced gardeners; others are so easy and pest free they can be grown by anyone, nearly anywhere.

This collection of pots shows repetition as well as variety. Different terra-cotta pots work well together because the red of the begonia and geraniums match.

Bright colors are not always required, as this perennial sedum with white sweet alyssum at its base demonstrates.

IN A CONTAINER OR IN THE GROUND?

Advantages of plants grown in the ground:

- They don't have to be watered as often.
- Roots in the ground are better insulated from dramatic swings in temperature
- Roots can grow farther in search of nutrients.
- Plants are more likely to reach their natural size, and flower and fruit better.

Disadvantages of plants grown in the ground:

- There is only one good shot at soil preparation.
- They are stuck where they are planted—for better or worse.
- Severe weather or sudden changes can damage or kill them.
- Pests, especially those that damage roots, are hard to avoid.
- You have to go to them, to see and enjoy them.

Advantages of growing plants in containers:

- Choices of plants you can grow side by side from all over the world is unlimited.
- You can change or control the environmental conditions the plants are grown in.
- Plants are portable, so you can move them to better growing conditions if needed.
- Plants can be isolated from one another if pests begin to build up.
- You can move faded or dying plants out of view or to a "recovery" area.
- Plants are closer to you, so you can enjoy them better.

Disadvantages of growing plants in containers:

- Though easy to grow, potted plants require regular if not constant care.
- Dripping or seeping water and fertilizer can damage decks, patios, or floors.
- Some plants have to be moved indoors and outdoors seasonally.
- Container plants are often more short lived than in-ground plants.

. . . it is better to determine what kind of growing conditions your home or garden offers and find plants that do well there.

In addition, where you place the pots will have a great impact—for better or worse—on how the plants thrive. Even with extensive horticulture knowledge and the very best care, location alone can determine whether the plants will survive. This may even change during the different seasons.

Finally, there are many opportunities for growing more plants from the ones you already have. Some plants are very easy to propagate by saving seed, rooting stem cuttings, or dividing roots. Propagating plants often becomes a special way to share with family or friends.

FIRST THINGS FIRST: Plants usually grow better in the ground—if, that is, they are in their native or very similar climate, and naturally get the right amount of sunlight, rain, nutrients, and temperatures. But if you choose to grow plants from a vastly different part of the country or world, you will have to do your best to mimic those growing conditions in your home or garden.

Still, there are several advantages for and against growing plants in the ground or in containers. You must weigh these against your willingness and ability to take care of potted plants.

Environmental and Cultural Needs

Though most plants are fairly adaptable and will tolerate surprising swings in growing conditions, every single one has its preferred needs and limits. Environmental conditions—the existing situation in your home or garden that affect the way plants grow—include the amount of sun or shade, temperature, humidity, and soil. Cultural requirements—what you do to keep plants growing—include watering and fertilization. Maintenance needs vary widely from plant to plant, and include pruning, pest control, winter protection, and the like.

Rather than trying to grow every plant your heart desires, which means attempting to change the growing conditions to meet a diverse group of plants, it is better to determine what kind of growing conditions your home or garden offers and find plants that do well there.

Light

Plants get their energy from the sun. Some grow and flower best when they get all-day sun; others do better with only seven or eight hours daily. A few are native to woods or jungles, and require shade or they will burn in mid-day sun; many of these will tolerate early morning or late afternoon sun, but will need watering more often.

The north side of a house or wall is usually shady all year; south-facing walls and windows get sun all day every day, unless they are shaded by large plants. Choose sun-loving plants for southern exposures, or place their containers under the shade of larger plants or a few feet back from south-facing windows.

In general, eastern exposures (morning sun) are cooler than western exposures with hot afternoon sun.

All of this, of course, is also dependent on where you garden. Coastal climates are often overcast part of the day and are cooler than inland areas, and normally shade-loving plants can grow in more sun. Also, nearby lights, even security lighting outdoors, can prevent some plants from getting the night rest they need, which affects their ability to flower.

Understanding your container plant's cultural and environmental requirements leads to plants as healthy and beautiful as this hydrangea.

CAN'T MISS TIP:

GIVE EXTRA CARE

Plants grown above the ground in pots are exposed to more cold, radiated heat, and drying wind than plants in the ground. Cluster or group plants for shared humidity, and be prepared to move plants as needed if environmental conditions change.

You will have success with many plants in any of these sun or shade conditions, and fail with others. Play around with your choices until you find those that grow best for you with the least amount of worry about sun or shade.

Temperature

Most plants have a fairly wide range of temperature tolerance, within certain extremes. Although most gardeners in America know that many popular potted plants will freeze to death if left outside in the winter, there are many exceptions, especially in the milder regions such as the middle to lower South, Florida, Southwest, and the Mediterranean areas that hug the coastal areas of our West Coast.

In addition, a lot of very hardy outdoor shrubs, small trees, and perennials can survive the winter in containers left outside in all but the most extreme winter areas, especially if they are clustered together out of direct exposure, then watered and mulched before really cold weather sets in. Keep in mind that ice draws water away from roots, and cold can penetrate containers much more readily than it can frozen ground.

Note that much winter cold damage is caused by desiccation, leaves and stems drying out in cold wind while roots are dormant and unable to supply the plant with water. Protect plants from desiccation by wrapping them in sheets or moving them out of the wind. To help potted plants get through the winter in northern states, bury pots up to their rims in the ground, tie up their branches, and wrap them in burlap or a chicken wire sheath filled with straw. It's a lot of work, but it can be done.

In addition to during extreme cold, most plants shut down when the temperatures get above the mid-90s, unable to draw moisture from their roots as quickly as it evaporates from leaves. Move plants out of direct sun during prolonged hot spells, and water a little more frequently (but don't overwater, which can rot roots or cause disease).

Humidity

In addition to absorbing light and converting it into plant energy, leaves are the "air conditioners" of plants, and they regulate how much water that roots need to absorb. During hot, dry, and windy weather, leaves can lose moisture more rapidly than roots can take it up from the soil. Some plants are well adapted to these conditions, including cacti, succulents, plants with needle-like foliage, or those that wilt naturally during the day but pick back up at night.

However, most popular potted plants thrive when the humidity is high, which reduces the rate at which leaf moisture evaporates. Indoors, avoid placing container plants in direct drafts from central air conditioning and heating ducts; outdoors, place containers near turf or groundcover areas that produce humidity, and away from exposed concrete patios or driveways.

How to Increase Humidity

Increase humidity around plants by clustering them together to create a "microclimate" of shared humidity, much like that found in natural plant communities. This works equally well outdoors as indoors, but is usually more crucial indoors where air conditioners and furnaces are constantly at work removing humidity.

When the weather is cold, remember to protect your plants.

CAN'T MISS TIP:

STERILIZING SOIL

Sterilizing garden soil sounds like a great idea, but it is not that great to actually do. Baking or steaming dirt is time-consuming and extremely malodorous. If you want to add real dirt to your potting soil, just buy bagged topsoil, which is usually already sterilized for weed seeds.

Soil

It is no secret that potted plants grow poorly when their containers are filled with just plain dirt. The soil your plants grow in determines what kind of roots they will have. Good soil equals good roots; bad soil can actually kill roots.

Soil serves several basic functions. It not only helps keep plants from falling over, but holds water, nutrients, and crucial air that roots need to breathe. Plants grown in regular soil in the garden can usually send roots to wherever they can get the air and water they need, but potted plants are stuck in whatever soil you plant them in.

A great soil
- is sturdy enough to support plants.
- has readily available nutrients.
- holds water a fairly long time for roots, but drains excess water out quickly.
- has lots of small spaces for air to be pulled in around roots.

The soil requirements for these two planters are different because of their sizes and the plants in them.

■ holds nutrients so fertilizer lasts as long as possible before washing out.

■ is not contaminated with weed seed, insects, or disease organisms.

Most natural soil is made of tiny clay or sand particles that pack down and lose porosity (the all-important spaces that hold water and air for plant roots). As the soil gets watered over and over, it tends to pack down in containers, so water has a hard time percolating in. Once wet, native soil generally stays wet for too long, then dries into hard mud.

For this reason, gardeners have long added very common ingredients to their soils for growing plants in containers, which is called potting soil. The most common amendment material added is organic matter such as compost or manure; finely ground bark; or peat moss, a fluffy, long-lasting, sponge-like material made from decomposed mosses dug out of dried-out peat bogs. Other ingredients include coarse or "sharp" sand (not river sand, which is too fine and sugary, and is often contaminated with weed seeds and pests); crunchy perlite, a natural volcanic ash that has been superheated and fluffed up like popcorn; and vermiculite, a flaky type of mineral that, like perlite, is popped and expanded by high heat.

Special wetting agents can be added to potting soils to help water penetrate throughout the soil mix. Moisture-retentive gels are available which, when mixed with potting soil, swell up as they absorb water, to be slowly released during dry periods. Sometimes charcoal is added to potting soils to absorb gases and smells from decomposing potting soil.

Many brands of potting soil mixes are available at garden centers, some better than others. Store-bought mixes are highly variable between brands: Some have too much peat that stays wet too long, and others have too much bark that drains and dries out quickly. Sometimes a potting soil company will put almost identical mixes in different bags, so it is a good idea to open a bag slightly to make sure you are getting what you want.

In general, you get what you pay for. Look for a potting soil that is both well drained yet holds water in smaller pore spaces; it will have a good bit

CAN'T MISS TIPS:

SOIL FOR THE POT

In general, potting soils in large pots require more coarse materials for better drainage, while small pots and hanging baskets can use a lighter mix (even though they have to be watered more often). Cacti and succulents need more sand or perlite. Special potting soils are available for specialty plants such as orchids, African violets, and others.

CEC

The "sticky" ability of some soil ingredients to grab and hold nutrients for plant roots to absorb later is called cation exchange capacity or CEC. Peat moss, vermiculite, compost, and manure have a high CEC, while sand, perlite, and bark have poor CEC. It is best to use some of each.

of fluffy peat moss, and at least a little perlite or bark for drainage.

Commercial-grade soil mixes are often very good for growing plants quickly to sell them, but they often dry out too fast in the home garden; most plants grown this way need repotting into a better, more long-lasting soil mix.

Keep bags of potting soil closed to keep the soil from drying out or getting contaminated with insects or disease organisms. Leaving bags of potting soil out in the weather can cause the plastic to degrade or allow potting soil to get wet in the rain.

Mix Your Own

Home-made potting soil is easy and economical, and you can customize it to fit the needs of your particular plants or your personal watering habits (the more you like to water, the more important the soil's drainage should be). It will also be more consistent, because you choose the ingredients yourself rather than wonder what's in a sealed bag.

You can make an inexpensive, general potting soil fluffier by mixing it with finely ground bark or perlite. A little topsoil or sand will make a light mix heavier.

A totally homemade mix can be created with just a little experimentation; what you are looking for is a mix that is consistent from batch to batch, provides good drainage and air spaces, and holds water and nutrients. Some options:

■ SIMPLE MIX: Use one part peat moss and one part of either perlite, vermiculate, sand, or bark, plus a little lime.

■ FOR A LIGHT MIX, use two parts peat moss, one part sand, one part perlite, and a little lime.

■ FOR A HEAVIER MIX, use one part peat moss, two parts bark, one part sand, and a little lime.

■ FOR CONTAINER TREES AND SHRUBS, use the heavier mix plus one part sterilized topsoil.

Good potting soil can be made, if you have the right ingredients. Clockwise, from top: Peat moss, bark, vermiculite, perlite, fertilizer beads, finished potting soil mix.

Common Potting Soil Ingredients

These are the most common potting soil ingredients:

- **PEAT MOSS:** Dried, decomposed moss that both fluffs up potting soils and absorbs and holds water and nutrients for plant roots; lasts a long time, but is acidic.
- **FINELY GROUND BARK:** Inexpensive material that adds bulk to potting soils (like adding crumbled crackers to a bowl of soup) and increases drainage and air spaces.
- **COMPOST OR MANURE:** Completely decomposed, natural materials that give "life" to potting soil, while enriching it with valuable nutrients and beneficial bacteria and fungi for better root growth.
- **PERLITE:** White, crunchy material made from superheated volcanic ash that bulks up soils and provides very important air spaces and drainage.
- **VERMICULITE:** Puffed mineral flakes that increase drainage while holding nutrients for roots to absorb.
- **LIMESTONE:** Natural material used in moderation to reduce acidity of potting soils.
- **COARSE SAND:** Used to add weight to potting soils and increase drainage somewhat.
- **TOPSOIL:** A select grade of soil that has been sterilized to kill weed seeds and pests, and both provides and helps hold nutrients.
- **OTHERS:** Old sawdust, coconut fiber (used as a peat substitute), and rice hulls.

To get a really good blend of ingredients, pile them on the driveway or other hard, smooth surface (put the lightest ingredients on the bottom, so the heavier ones can work their way down). Using a flat spade or shovel, go in a circle, around and around, mixing it a little at a time until it is all perfectly well blended. Store it in a plastic trashcan with a lid to keep bugs and other stuff out.

Water

Without water, all life ceases; too much water is nearly as bad. Either can happen quickly to plants in pots. The size of your containers, your potting soil mix, and the choice of plants all affect how often you will need to water—or not water.

CAN'T MISS TIP:

HOW MUCH LIME?

As peat moss and bark decompose, they release natural acids, which can interfere with the ability of plants to absorb certain nutrients. To neutralize the acids, add ground-up limestone (available at garden centers in small amounts) at the rate of about one pound (a pint) of limestone to a large trashcan full of potting soil mix, or half a pound (a cup) per large wheelbarrow load.

If your pots are small, or your potting soil is too well drained, you may find yourself having to water a lot more often than you want, and your plants will risk suffering from your neglect. If your pot is large, your potting soil poorly drained, there is an increased risk of roots drowning and rotting from too much water for too long.

Yet there is no universal time or method for watering. Anyone who waters routinely, without taking into account the temperature, wind, type of plants, amount of fertilizer, or other factors that affect the rate at which water is or is not used by plants, is risking the plant's health.

Plants grown in full sun will of course need watering more often than those in the shade. The same goes for windy conditions or hot weather, both of which dry potted plants out quickly. Plants grown in light-colored pots, which reflect light and therefore heat, are less likely to need watering than those in dark, heat-absorbing colors. The type of potting soil you use can be a strong factor in how fast or slowly it dries out; soils with more perlite and bark will dry out more quickly than those with more soil or compost.

Also, some plants naturally need watering more often, especially those with large thin leaves, compared with plants with thick or fleshy leaves or very small or needle-like foliage. Very young or recently repotted plants will need more careful attention to watering. And plants that are very root-bound, having less potting soil to hold moisture, will need watering nearly constantly.

There are all sorts of ways to water container-grown plants, from simply aiming the hose at them to sophisticated drip irrigation systems. Sometimes the choice depends on how many pots you have to water, because dragging around a hose can be quite a chore.

Using a general sprinkler like at garden centers is very inefficient and wasteful, and you have little control over how much water every individual plant gets. Plus, as water splashes onto foliage, it creates ideal conditions for diseases to spread and develop.

The most common way to water, especially indoors, is by hand, using a hand-held watering can

Overwatering can lead to stinky, rotten roots.

or a special hose set-up hooked to the sink faucet. You can determine how much and how long to water each plant, without spilling water or causing pots to overflow. Hose attachments with extensions for hanging baskets, different sprinkler heads, and hose-end shut off valves all help make this more efficient and pleasant. Try to not overwater or water so forcefully it compacts the soil or splashes soil out of the pot.

Drip or trickle irrigation is not very attractive to look at, but it is extremely water-conservative—a very important consideration in arid areas where water is a precious commodity and where a small amount of constant moisture is difficult to achieve by hand watering. It's also a better choice now that the components have gotten very inexpensive. Drip irrigation is a system of flexible pipes, a main one with a filter and pressure regulator that carries water from the faucet, and which has many smaller ones that branch off and go to individual containers. It delivers very small amounts of water at a time, steadily, which keeps soils moist without oversaturating.

Your container plants will be happier and healthier if you water them when and as much as they need.

Drip systems have to be run for several hours at a time to work best, because it takes a very long time to get dry soils moist using drip irrigation. Large containers may need several drip emitters to get the job done. Raised bed gardens may be watered more practically with the use of soaker hoses that ooze water along their entire length.

Self-watering pots, which use wicks to pull water from a reservoir to keep potting soil moist, work well for small pots and for the larger kinds used in urban malls and other large areas where regular watering is impractical. However, these containers often have a problem with fertilizer buildups, because they can't be "leached" or flushed out easily. It is also difficult to monitor how much water a plant gets, which can lead to drying out or overwatering.

CAN'T MISS
TIP:

WATER TWICE

Water potted plants twice—once to wet the peat moss so it will expand tightly against the side of the pot, and a second time a few minutes later to really let it soak in. Sometimes this will cut your watering frequency by a third as often or more.

How Often Should Plants Be Watered?

The water needs of plants change from season to season and with the weather, which automatic systems cannot take into consideration. You have to adjust them as needed. There are easy ways to tell if and when a potted plant needs watering; note that some of the following may also indicate a poor or damaged root system caused by improper watering.

■ It droops or wilts during the day, and does not perk up in the evening.

■ The plant looks off-color or "tired" or the outside of a clay pot looks dry.

■ You can't feel cool moisture when you stick your finger at least three inches deep in the potting soil (surfaces may be dry when in fact most of the soil is moist).

■ The pot feels light; lift it after watering to get a "feel" for its weight when full of water, then lift it regularly to see when it starts getting dry and light.

Water, fertilizer, sunshine—these rubber trees and caladiums have obviously received exactly what they require.

■ A moisture meter can give a "ballpark" idea of when soils are starting to dry out. Insert its long, needle-like probe deep into the soil and read its gauge.

In nearly every part of the country, especially in highly populated areas even where rainfall and water reservoirs are abundant, water shortages can be a problem, at least seasonally. There are many ways to reduce the amount of water a potted plant needs, and to save time for you. Here are a few:

■ Choose plants with lower water needs, and avoid those that are super thirsty.

■ Group pots together to raise humidity and reduce sunlight on sides of pots.

■ Use mulches on the soil surface to reduce the wicking effect of the sun.

■ Move pots into the shade when possible.

■ Install drip irrigation, which is very efficient and conserves water.

■ Use soil polymer gels that absorb water for plants to use between waterings.

■ Place potted plants into two pots, which reduces sunlight on the smaller pot, keeping soil cooler and moist.

■ Containers set on the ground can be partially sunk into the soil or surrounded with mulch, which also reduces temperature and the wicking effect. This works surprisingly well.

■ Don't allow weeds to grow in raised beds or large containers, because they are often greedy for water and can quickly dry out the soil.

Fertilizer

Plants need certain nutrients, some more than others, for healthy growth. Those grown in containers are utterly dependent on you as a gardener to feed them. Anyone who has ever neglected an old potted plant knows that it can get by for weeks or even months without being "fed," but it certainly won't be sturdy or perform as well.

CAN'T MISS TIPS:

KEEP DRAINAGE CLEAR

Pots with clogged drainage holes are plant killers. Roots, potting soil, or other debris can keep water from draining out of pots, which can lead to root drowning or even root rot. Check from time to time when you water to make sure excess water drains properly. You may need to stick something long and stiff through the potting soil and through the hole to clear clogs.

SOIL POLYMERS

Soil polymers are a bit like Jell-o—quickly absorbing many times their weight and volume in water. The difference comes in that they slowly release it. A soil polymer can be mixed with potting soil, or put in a cup, watered until it swells up, and placed upside down over the potting soil, so as it loses its hold on water, the moisture goes into the soil.

Different plants have varying needs for fertilizers. Flowering, fruiting, or rapidly growing plants need fertilizing more than others. Annuals and hanging baskets—which get watered more often than large containers or slower-growing perennial and woody plants—need more fertilizer because it has dissolved and been washed away more frequently. Some potting soils have very low cation exchange capacity, which limits the amount of fertilizer they hold between waterings.

Plant Nutrients in a Nutshell

Plants need different elements in different amounts. The "big three" of nitrogen, phosphorus, and potassium are most important—they are the meat, potatoes, and vegetables of the plants world. However, others are just as important for container-grown plants, which cannot forage outside their pots for the nutrients they need. Calcium, iron, zinc, magnesium, and a handful of others are called micronutrients or trace elements, because they are needed in very small amounts.

It is very important to use a fertilizer at least every now and then that contains these. All fertilizers have the ingredients listed on their labels, by percentage, as indicated by the three numbers on the container label.

■ NITROGEN, the first ingredient, is necessary for green growth, but does not last very long and needs applying more often than the others.

- PHOSPHORUS, the second number, helps flowering and fruiting plants be more productive, though it does not "cause" flowers or fruits. It lasts in the soil and does not need to be applied very often.
- POTASSIUM, the third ingredient, helps with overall plant growth, stiffens stems, and has many other functions. It also lasts a long time in soils.
- MICRONUTRIENTS SUCH AS IRON, ZINC, COPPER, AND CALCIUM are minerals used by plants in very small amounts, to help major nutrients work better—just like vitamins in diet. Because they wash away easily, they should be applied to potting soils fairly regularly.

Regular deadheading helps ensure flowers continue to bloom.

Types of Fertilizer Formulations

Fertilizers come in several forms, each with pros and cons. "Balanced" fertilizers usually contain only the main nutrients needed by plants, while "complete" fertilizers have everything plants need to flourish, including the major and minor elements.

Organic fertilizers are those made from natural ingredients, and are less likely to burn or overfeed plants. Specialty fertilizers are formulated for specific plants, such as African violets, citrus, tomato, and others; they are often mostly marketing glitz—not necessarily bad, just expensive.

Here are a few types of fertilizers.

- DRY OR GRANULAR FERTILIZERS dissolve over time depending on how much water they are exposed to. They are generally very inexpensive.
- WATER-SOLUBLE OR LIQUID FERTILIZERS are absorbed very quickly by plant roots and even into leaves (foliage feeding), but do not last very

long and have to be used regularly. When used regularly, they are relatively expensive, plus they take time and effort to mix and use.

■ SLOW-RELEASE FERTILIZER BEADS are filled with fertilizer that with every watering dissolves and washes into the soil. They are fairly expensive, but extremely efficient and save time.

■ FERTILIZER STICKS are just hard variations on dry or granular fertilizers. They make sense to people, but not to plants which need fertilizer spread evenly over the entire potting soil, not just here and there. Break the sticks into small pieces and poke them into the soil.

Maintenance

Just like picking up clothes, washing dishes, and all the other little chores we do, there are some simple tricks to keeping potted plants up and running.

Don't forget to weed. Dandelions and other weeds like growing in a container as well as they do in your yard.

If ignored, they can certainly cause the plants to look ragged or fail to perform well.

■ CHANGING OUT PLANTS: seasonally getting rid of the old plants and replacing with new ones. This is usually done twice a year—once for warm-season or summer plants, and again in the fall to have cool-season or winter plants to enjoy.

■ DEADHEADING: pinching or pruning of faded flowers, which prevents them from making seeds and frustrates the plants into new flowering growth.

■ LEACHING: flushing out built-up and unused nutrients from potting soils and containers. Do this by watering very thoroughly, which dissolves the old fertilizer "salts," then water again until water flows from the bottom drainage hole.

■ PRUNING: done for size control, to get rid of excess or wayward growth, and to remove diseased, or dead growth. It can be done any time it is needed. Heavy pruning may cause a temporary setback on flowering plants.

- REPOTTING: moving overgrown, old, or rootbound plants as needed. Gently tap the plant out of its old pot, and replant in the next size larger pot.

- ROOT PRUNING: a way to keep plants from growing too large or fast. It simply means pulling plants out of their containers, cutting a few of the crowded or excess roots, and putting the plants back into their containers with a little fresh potting soil.

- TURNING POTS: rotating pots every few weeks, usually a quarter of a turn, which keeps all sides of the plants exposed to the amount of light they need. Without this, plants can get leggy or bare on one side.

- WINTER PROTECTION: bringing potted plants indoors or into a greenhouse or garage, or grouping them in a protected place outdoors and covering them with mulch.

CAN'T MISS TIP:

WHEN TO REPOT

Repot plants when they are dormant or their growth is slowest, not when they are in full swing with flowering or fruiting. This often involves cutting roots, which generally is best to do in the season opposite when the plants are at their peak of growth (repot fall bloomers in the spring and spring bloomers in the fall). When repotting large plants, let them dry out a bit first, so their roots shrink and the plants are easier to pull out of their pots.

Pest Control

This is an ever-changing area, far too complicated to cover in this book. Best bets for pest control include:

- Identify the pest (bug, disease, whatever) accurately—take it to your country Extension Service office for an agent or a Master Gardener to examine, because sometimes untrained garden center employees will try to sell you unnecessary products.

- Try washing or light pruning to get rid of the problem pest.

- Easy-to-use natural pesticides include pyrethrins, derived from a type of chrysanthemum; insecticidal soaps, which smother small, soft-bodied pests such as aphids and whiteflies without harming beneficial insects; Neem, an oil from a tropical tree with amazing pesticidal qualities, but harmless to people and most beneficial insects; strips of copper wire, which can help deter slugs and snails.

- If a pesticide is needed, consider the risks, the expense, and the likelihood of success. Choose a natural control over a chemical one.

- Encourage beneficial insects and other critters such as toads and lizards, which eat bad guys.

- Apply pesticides only to the target pests, not to the entire garden.
- Always read and follow all label directions when choosing, mixing, and applying pesticides—even natural or organic ones.
- Plant in the right location and water and fertilize properly to encourage healthy growth, not fast, rank growth.
- Maintain a diverse planting of container plants, which discourages pests in the first place, and helps reduce the target population.

Propagation

Growing new plants from parts of another is a fascinating way to get more plants both for your own garden and to share with others. Potted plants have been "pass-along" plants for many centuries, and need not be very complicated. Here are a few of the easier ways to propagate plants.

There are several ways to start new plants, but they all result in being able to share with your friends.

- AIR LAYERING: a type of cutting in which the stem being rooted is only partly severed from the "mother" plant, with a toothpick or other small object stuck in the cut to keep it from healing over, then the cut area wrapped with moist sphagnum moss or potting soil in a plastic wrap. After roots form in the plastic-wrapped moss, the cutting can be completely removed and planted in its own pot.
- DIRECT SEEDING: sowing seeds onto moist, preferably sterile or special seed-starting soils, then keeping them moist, warm, and humid until the new plants sprout and get large enough to transplant. Do not sow seeds too thickly, or the young plants will be crowded and more prone to disease problems. Transplant excess plants when they are large enough to have two or three sets of "true" leaves. Be gentle.
- DIVIDING: digging crowded, multi-stem plants out of their pots, cutting them into individual plants, each with a piece of stem and some roots, and replanting into separate containers. This is often done on clump-forming plants such as ferns, canna, and mint. Note: This is best done when plants are not in active growth or flowering.

■ LEAF PROPAGATION: a unique way to propagate some plants. Jade, African violets, night-blooming cereus, and some begonias can grow roots and new plants from the base of mature leaves that are stuck into moist soil.

■ ROOTING IN SOIL: easily done on leggy or stemmy plants such as tomatoes, most tropical plants, roses, chrysanthemums, and the like. Cut off stems that are young but mature enough to be firm, strip the bottom few leaves from the stem, and insert them into moist potting soil. Keep moist and out of direct sunshine for a few weeks, until roots form (you can tell by gently tugging on the cuttings—if they "tug back," they are rooting).

■ ROOTING IN WATER: can be done with quite a few tropical plants, including coleus and ornamental sweet potatoes. Cut mature stems, strip off the leaves from one or two leaf joints, and place the bottom portion of the stem (with the cut off leaf joints in fresh water. It often only takes a few days or a couple of weeks for roots to start forming.

All plants need the basics of life, from sunshine and water to fertilizer and tolerable temperatures. Your selection of containers, plants, and settings can make or break your plants, but many problems can be overcome with attention to regular feeding, pest control, and other simple gardening techniques.

Don't let your plants be victims—help them be survivors!

> *Growing new plants from parts of another is a fascinating way to get more plants both for your own garden and to share with others.*

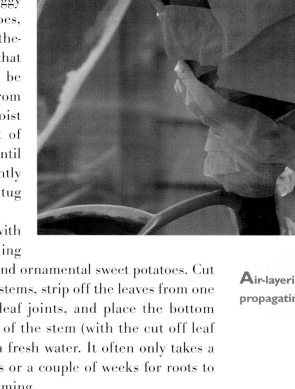

Air-layering is one form of propagating your plants.

Putting It All Together

regardless of what current "tastemakers" say, arranging plants and containers is less popular science and more personal choice—just like selecting a wardrobe or choosing a hairstyle. So the very idea that design has anything to do with growing plants in containers may seem a little pretentious; mostly we just plop plants into pots and stick them wherever they seem to fit best. But once you start to move them around for better views, or to create a different "look"—or begin combining different plants in the same pots, or even matching the plants to the pot (or vice versa)—you are getting involved in design.

Whether you need a single bold plant and container for a strong visual focal point, or you find yourself creating a lush tropical or formal classical effect, mixing plants, containers, and their settings can be as thrilling as growing the plants themselves.

Set Your Goals

It won't take you long to catch on that container gardens can be used to bring to life your every gardening wish, sometimes better than in-ground plants.

Throughout history, potted plants have been used in some of the same ways all over the world, in all cultures. Whether for growing just one special plant, arranging multiple containers of plants, or grouping several plants in one container, they make it easy to create seasonal highlights, grow plants where plants normally don't grow, divide areas of the landscape, and accessorize the garden.

Some of the most common goals in designing with container plants include getting the most out of your combinations visually, for as long as possible, and with the least amount of maintenance or "downtime." The style of both containers and plants has an immense effect on how things look, but choosing plants carefully for a site—in addition to how well you take care of them—can make or break their performance and, ultimately, your satisfaction.

With container gardens, you can create strong accents, tone down boring walls or fences, add colorful zest to a patio in every season, create miniature slices of formality or naturalistic areas, and even bring the garden indoors during inclement weather. It's not only possible, but actually easy to grow attractive edibles—herbs, vegetables, fruits, and flowers—close to the house, without a lot of backbreaking work. It is even possible to have a small spot of turfgrass in a pot, like a pet lawn that is so much easier to care for than the full-blown deal.

Whether you are starting from scratch in a new garden or adding to an existing mature garden, there are several easy but important considerations, all routinely kept in mind by professional designers—almost like recipes for success. Of course many great gardeners do things with gusto

These *Euryops chrysanthemoides* are perfect for this decorative container.

DIFFERENT GARDEN DESIGNS

You can accomplish many of the same things with container gardens as you can with in-ground plants. A container garden can

- Create garden themes such as Oriental, cottage, formal, tropical, and so on.
- Perform as accents or focal points to draw the eye upward, or toward good views or away from less desirable views.
- Draw lines in the landscape just like hedges or walks.
- Visually "connect the dots" with rhythm through repetition.
- Wall off areas to create new garden spaces or for foot traffic control.
- Mass groups to take up space, much like groundcovers.
- Brighten dull areas or tone down "busy" or cluttered areas.
- Bring color, fragrance, texture, form, and other sensory elements, both indoors and out.

In addition, potted plants can become soothing or challenging hobbies for people who like attention to detail. Hobby plants range from collections of many different kinds of one plant (African violets, orchids or bromeliads, miniature roses, tropicals, ferns, and so on) to focused attention on highly detailed plants such as bonsai or topiary.

Plants in pots make it easier to have a crucial connection with nature for people who have little room or ability to garden outside, and as therapy for those who can use more closeness with a living creature—one not quite as demanding as an animal pet!

in exactly the opposite direction from tried-and-true methods, and enjoy their gardens all the more. But one thing is true: The more you understand the basics of good design, the easier it will be to successfully break the rules.

Container plantings don't always have to be serious; sometimes you can just have fun!

The Right Place

The first main consideration for good design with containers is to have a good overview of your landscape or garden in the first place. How your garden is situated regarding sun or shade (in the winter as well as in the summer, as light changes with every season) and the general climate in your area of the country will determine to some extent what kinds of plants will grow best, in which seasons, and requiring how much care. Even the architecture and colors of your home and other "nonnegotiable" hard features and accessories will play a role in how you choose materials and plants for containers.

Work with what you already have. Whether you like formal or informal, flowers or foliage, food or fun, use container plants to complement your home and garden, and your life, not compete with it or add to your already busy schedule.

Creating Garden Rooms

Any space can be divided into smaller areas, using and moving around containers just as you rearrange furniture in a big room to change the feel and flow. There are many different types, themes, and moods of gardens, from formal with straight lines and a limited number of plant types, to tropical areas, private areas, places to relax, and working areas. Container plants can be chosen and arranged to help create the right feel or effect, especially in small areas where in-ground shrubs and trees may be less versatile.

Focal points are those areas where you want to attract attention. Large containers with shrubs or small trees, especially those pruned into tight topiaries, all but grab visitors by the eyes. The same effect can be accomplished with a bold combination of pots with bold flowers or foliage. These should ideally be as attractive year-round as possible.

Entryways are excellent places for focal point combinations of potted plants, and can be changed out seasonally if needed. Blank walls on the house or a fence can be toned down by using groups of wall hanging pots or carefully placed hanging baskets.

Decks or patios can be easily adorned with small groups of potted plants, which can also serve as warnings for people who may wander too close to a drop-off. Potted plants can also lead the eye toward and down or up steps;

Although the canna has one bright orange flower, the main attraction of the container is the foliage. Situated in front of a stone wall, the planting is a real eye-catcher.

Consider these two important design principles for getting started using containers effectively:

1. Contrasting or Compatible Lines: Any landscape has many existing "lines"—roofline, windows, walks, fences, and so on—that can either be accented with formal planters and tightly pruned plants repeated for effect, or toned down with informal groups of roundish containers overstuffed with loose arrangements of bold tropical plants. An added benefit of having less regimented plantings is that if something dies, few people will notice!

2. The Big View: How and where can container plants be used as major elements of your landscape? Can a row of large containers be used like a low hedge or screen? Would a well-built raised bed serve double duty as seating near a patio? Is there a view you need to tone down using hanging baskets? Is there a landscape style, color scheme, or other effect that can be enhanced with both the containers and the plants in them?

The idea is that container gardens can easily and quickly be used to add to, not detract from, your entire landscape and its elements.

the use of very light-colored flowers or variegated foliage can even reduce the need for night lighting near unexpected steps.

Small space gardens can be walled off from other areas with a row of medium-sized or large containers, especially those planted with tall evergreen shrubs, small trees, vines on a trellis, or tropical plants. Plant stands that resemble bookcases can be used as outdoor "walls" of potted plants. Arranging hanging baskets in tiers hung at varying heights can also provide a sense of enclosure or privacy.

Rooftop gardens have become sensational in cities where space is at a premium. Large containers filled with lightweight potting soils can not only bring greenery and color to an otherwise bare scene, but also have a cooling effect on the area all around it.

These plantings help define the patio area and add privacy.

The Right Plant

Whether you use potted plants for valuable design elements of the larger landscape; as a transition from one area to another (including from indoors to outside); or up close on a deck, patio, or balcony for a more intimate viewing and use, it is worth considering which plants you choose and what you grow them in. Otherwise plants may suffer or die (or worse to some designers, clash with your other décor).

For plants that will be up close and personal, especially those in containers on decks, patios, containers, or indoors, choose those with interesting

This grouping of pots with annuals and houseplants brightens the corner of a patio.

details such as pretty or fragrant flowers, unusual stems and leaves (variegated or interesting shapes), edible parts, and colors that make you want to look more closely. Especially good are those that flower in the morning or in the evening, when you are more likely to want to be outside. Avoid plants with lots of stickers, rambling growth that can grab passersby, or weird odors, or ones that attract butterflies (which usually mean they also attract bees—not fun to be close to!).

Also avoid those that look less than ideal part of the year because of insect or disease problems, or that have to be sprayed—who wants to relax outside on a deck with a plant that smells like poison?

For plants to be used as enticements to pull you or your visitors out of the house or off the patio and into the garden, choose lush foliage, big flowers, and colors that complement something inside the house. The farther you get from a window or patio area, the more important it will be for plants and their containers to be big and bold—remember, some people wear bifocals, and need extra prodding to look beyond their noses!

Compatible Plants and Pots

No doubt you already have, or will quickly acquire, a taste for what looks good growing in what kind of container. Selecting a container made of the right material and in the right color and size to go with your house, architecture, garden, or personal tastes is one thing, and finding a plant that you just can't garden without is another. But when the two get together, you don't want an unexpected clash.

The farther you get from a window or patio area, the more important it will be for plants and their containers to be big and bold.

Bold/Tropical Foliage Plants
- Coleus, Aeonium, hosta, hoya, peperomia, philodendron, rubber tree, fatsia, Aucuba, caladium, canna, angel trumpet, banana, bromeliad, croton, elephant ears, fire spike, Hawaiian ti, sago, shell ginger, Aspidistra, dracaena, sweet potato vine, dusty miller, dumb cane, Chinese hibiscus, Persian shield

Roundy Plants
- Barrel cactus, hosta, rex begonia, sago, croton, bromeliad, scented geranium, basil, pentas, impatiens, diascia, boxwood, dwarf conifers, gardenia, dwarf roses, Bergenia, dumb cane, pentas, Chinese hibiscus, pelargonium

Spikey/upright Plants
- Salvia, aloe, dwarf conifers, Japanese bloodgrass, ponytail palm, snake plant, Aspidistra, dracaena, canna, hyacinth, bird of paradise, fire spike, shell ginger, Hawaiian ti, Mexican petunia, flowering tobacco, hollyhock, veronica, devil's backbone, lemon grass, chives, Chinese evergreen

Fillers
- Aster, scented geranium, Aeonium, impatiens, pentas, roses, dill, sage, parsley, daffodil, cigar plant, ixora, painted fern, chives, tarragon, ladies mantle, astilbe, cranesbill geranium, melampodium, lavender, coreopsis, ivy, catmint, daylily, scarlet sage, candytuft, yarrow, nandina

Cascading
- Ivy, sweet pea, scaevola, licorice plant, lobelia, diascia, nasturtium, petunia, dichondra, verbena, mint, hens and chicks, dianthus, wandering jew, spider plant, cranesbill geranium, burro tail, sweet potato vine, moss rose, lobelia, wintercreeper euonymus

Hot, Sunny Areas
- Mandevilla, moonflower, barrel cactus, hens and chicks, kalanchoe, daylily, melampodium, petunia, pentas, aloe, basil, chives, canna, daffodil, lavender, ixora, banana, citrus, croton, sago, amaryllis, roses, boxwood, moss rose, mum, sedum, ornamental pepper, lemon grass, aloe, aster, Japanese blood grass

Shade
- Coleus, geranium, impatiens, ivy, dichondra, Swedish ivy, Japanese maples, gardenia, coral bells, painted fern, hosta, scented geraniums, Agapanthus, caladium, bromeliads, orchids, fire spike, African violet, fatsia, Aucuba, staghorn fern, snake plant, Chinese evergreen, Aspidistra, shell ginger, tuberous begonias

Outdoors in Winter
- Ivy, aster, daylily, lavender, parsley, dwarf conifers, primroses, hollyhock, yarrow, sedum, arborvitae, wintercreeper euonymus

Beginner/Kids' Gardens
- Coleus, ivy, morning glory, sweet potato vine, dwarf roses, petunia, pentas, gloriosa daisy, daylily, hosta, painted fern, wandering jew, philodendron, snake plant, caladium, daffodil, grape hyacinth, hyacinth, Chinese evergreen, elephant ears, dusty miller, Joseph's coat, zinnia, sedum, lemon balm, begonias, nasturtium

Match your containers and plants with their backgrounds.

Here are a few easy guidelines to help make choices simpler than going on gut feelings alone:

■ Size matters. Choose a container the right scale for your garden—not too small to be overlooked, not too large to impose.

■ Make sure the plant fits in the container without getting lost or without growing so large it'll have to be repotted soon or tip over in a gust of wind.

■ If you use different kinds of containers, especially if you mix sizes and shapes, try to keep to one material or style.

■ Match your containers and plants with their backgrounds—a rustic wood deck may need natural-looking plants; contemporary settings can use a single bold plant and unusual pot. A formal garden is more relaxing if plain containers are used with clipped shrubs.

■ Or forget the color wheel and its rules—please yourself on this one, and simply remove what doesn't make you feel good when you look at it.

Color Wheel at a Glance

Primary colors are red, blue, and yellow, and are equidistant from one another on the color wheel, with all other colors gradually blending from one to the other in various shades. How you mix and match them will create vastly different effects. Here are some useful tips.

■ Use the primary colors together for bright, cheerful contrasts.

■ For vibrant looks, choose complementary colors (those opposite one another on the wheel).

■ For compatible combinations, choose harmonious colors (near one another on the wheel).

■ Create a soothing style using variations or shades of the same color.

■ Warm colors (red, orange, yellow) add pizzazz to a combination, and fool the eye into thinking the plants are closer to you than they really are.

■ Cool colors and pastels add a calmness to plant collections, and seem to recede from view.

■ Whites and grays work with all colors, and can have a calming and unifying effect.

■ Always consider the effect of foliage, including variegated green, yellow, and white, but don't overlook the value of burgundy, red, chartreuse, gold, and other foliage colors.

Never think that your own personal preferences are not "good enough"—few gardeners will ever agree on what looks good. Plant what you like, and if you don't like it later, change it. No big deal.

Even though the plant is usually tall when the pot is tall, these *Haworthia* are the perfect size for the strawberry pot.

This container of geraniums and lobelia proves that red and purple look great together.

Combining Shapes

Many gardeners really enjoy keeping things bold and simple—one plant to a pot: a stunning "main attraction" that celebrates its unique form, especially when set against a contrasting background, or one that simply gets too big and bulky to share its pot with anything else. This is a fantastic way to display unique plants and containers.

The planting in this Victorian urn is an example of an informal arrangement in a formal container, but it works because the spiky, roundy, and floppy plants look good together.

However, a growing trend is in mixing and matching plants, in the same container or in a group of containers, the same way flower arrangers and garden designers create arrangements with their flowers and landscape plants. They know that sometimes diversity has value, with plants helping one another make a more pleasing overall impression.

This is easier than most people realize, and doesn't have to be a cliché just because everyone seems to be doing it these days. Think about how a tall narrow tree will look better with smaller shrubs underplanted in groundcovers brimming with spring bulbs. The same principle works in container gardening as well.

Just as floral designers arrange flowers according to line, mass, and filler, garden designers often arrange plants according to an easy recipe using four basic shape plants:

■ SPIKY: usually tall and either narrow or with big bold leaves and flowers.

■ ROUNDY: generally as wide as it is tall, generally with tight foliage or flowers.

- FRILLY: light and airy, ferny, divided leaves or loosely arranged small flowers.
- FLOPPY: a tumbling, cascading flower, ground-cover, or vine.

To get started, select a tall or bold plant, and add a roundy plant or two. Between or around those, work in something frilly to weave it all together. Finish the buffet (if desired) with a touch of something that cascades over the pot rim and partway down, to tone down the overall composition.

Get it? This is oversimplified but it works, both in individual containers or in mixed groups of pots each with a different shape plant. Even the containers themselves can lend an air of "spiky" or "roundy"!

It is important to keep the changing season in mind so your "arrangement" holds up for as long as possible. Select plants that last the entire season, or be prepared to replace them as they lose their appeal or have other pots of plants ready to slip into the composition.

In addition, "hard" features and accessories can substitute for spiky or roundy plants. Think of a small "teepee" for vines in a pot, a round gazing globe, or a small statue set right in a large pot or in a pot set in with the others. Even a birdbath or bench can be used as a contrasting shape.

Of course, you can change the combination as you see fit, almost as easily as changing your mind about what you like or don't like.

The teepee in this arrangement creates the spiky element by providing a place for the black-eyed Susan vine to grow.

Form, Texture, and Proportion

Mixing and matching colors is fun, but there is more to the basics of design for gardeners who really want the right "look." Three of the most useful elements to know are form, texture, and proportion or scale.

Form is just the basic shape of a plant or pot—spiky, roundy, frilly are good examples. You can keep these all the same, or mix them up for a more interesting effect (see "Combining Shapes" earlier).

Texture is more difficult to define. Usually described as coarse, medium, or fine, it deals with the overall effect of a plant, mostly its leaves and flowers. Think of a fat, heavy cactus, a daylily or rose, and a fern, side by side,

KEEPING IT CLEAN

Containers can be messy. They tend to attract or collect fallen or blown debris in hard-to-reach areas between pots, and water and fertilizer seeps from drainage holes, even with saucers, and can stain decks or floors. Insects, weather, occasional neglect, and just plain end-of-season or old age can make them less attractive. Be prepared to move or replant a few as needed. Hint: Keep a "sickroom" area for recovering plants.

and you'll picture coarse, medium, and fine textures. Dark green round leaves look "heavier" than light green, as do large flowers compared with slender spikes of smaller flowers.

Proportion, or scale, has to do with how things look together size-wise. There's nothing wrong with tall plants beside smaller ones or big pots with small plants, but things usually look better, more natural, when they balance one another. Just as it takes a special sense of humor to place a miniature lighthouse or wishing well in a large front yard, it makes less sense to put a huge tropical plant in a tiny pot, or a mass of low-growing bulbs in a tall container.

This planting is a striking combination of textures. It works because the blue foliage of the agave is repeated in the Erigeron 'Sea Breeze', and the pink and wine colors of the Erigeron flowers and alumroot leaves are repeated in the agave spines.

The Right Plant for the Pot

Is there a "right" size plant for a pot? Not really, but most gardeners prefer plants that are a little taller than the pot they are growing in: any taller, and the pot may look overwhelmed or can tip over easily in wind. This doesn't always apply, of course—succulents or bonsai are often grown in very small pots, and tightly mounded plants can look good in low, wide containers. And trees, tree-form shrubs, grasses, and bamboo often look great in smaller pots. The main thing is not to lose little plants in large pots.

Here are some general guidelines for combining pots and plants.

■ Use containers of the same basic style or color, in varying sizes and shapes, perhaps with one different kind for a little visual "spice."

- Select a group of identical pots with identical plants for a stunning accent.
- Large pots and big groups of pots work well in large spaces; small groups work better up close.
- Small pots tend to go unnoticed or even neglected when stuck between larger ones.
- Mix plants of different shapes and sizes, but with the same basic growing needs.
- Include some pots that are taller than the others (or lift some up on bricks or risers).
- Scatter small groups of containers along walks or up steps for repetition.

Seasonal Highlights

Just as forcing bulbs to bloom out of season is a perfectly acceptable trick for bringing midwinter cheer to an otherwise gloomy season, container gardens offer gardeners many easy ways to have something to enjoy through all the seasons. Summer color is fairly easy to come by with annuals and perennials, but having color in the fall and winter requires planning.

By planning, you can plant spring bulbs in pots in the fall, and simply move them to wherever you want the show to be displayed when they come into bloom. Meanwhile, you can cut stems of spring-flowering shrubs when it may be snowing outside, and bring them indoors where they will sprout flowers. Tropical foliage plants offer year-round texture.

For quick color nearly any time of the year, tuck in annuals from a garden center, even for just a few days. For a year-round effect with containers, maintain at least some hardy evergreen plants such as conifers that provide the "bones" needed by even container gardens. If your winter is simply too severe for even those plants—remember, the roots of container plants are not insulated by soil, and even very cold-hardy plants can freeze or dry out in cold winter winds—then just leave the containers themselves out where they serve a reminders of warmer days past and future.

Similar containers hold similar plants. It makes for a simple but very effective display.

Another way to get the maximum color from flowers in pots is make sure they are fertilized (don't overdo it!), watered regularly, and deadheaded to keep more flowers coming on. Intermix colorful foliage with slower-blooming plants, and plant something with a strongly complementary color or form.

Accessorizing for Form or Fun

No matter how good a job you have done in applying the elements of design to choosing and matching plants and containers, sooner or later you will see the need or have an urge to add a "nonliving" accessory. It can be something as simple as choosing an ornate antique Victorian urn with metal wings to complete a scene, or as functional as adding a wooden or metal teepee for a vine to climb. Even something as practical as plant name labels can be chosen according to how they lend a special air to a container garden.

But sometimes a garden composition begs for something artistic—whether serious or whimsical—to give the right touch, to complete the scene, or to carry it through all the seasons. Gardeners often select these little additions to express themselves personally or to send a message or mood to others.

This is where the slippery slope of taste can get muddy. Some gardeners prefer life-size classical nude statues, while others are more comfortable with partly hidden gnome figurines. Choices run the gamut from cottage-like birdhouses to signs with garden quotes, from mirrors to gazing globes.

Plants used as annuals usually offer the most spectacular colors.

WATERING WANDS

A common watering wand with a shut-off valve at its base makes watering a real cinch, but be aware that long aluminum tubes and large "showerhead" emitters on some can be very heavy when filled with water, and can be stressful on tired wrists or arms.

Gardeners have little in common along these lines, and only the gardener—and his or her conscience, sense of propriety, or type of humor—are responsible for the results.

One thing for sure: Many gardens, both great and small, including container gardens, use accessories—artistic, gaudy, or otherwise. It's part of what makes gardening truly enjoyable.

Including a sculpture in a container can make a bland display into something immediately noticed.

Think Outside the Box

Special uses of containers make gardening much easier for young gardeners whose reach is not very long, as well as for gardeners who have trouble lifting, stooping, or moving around.

- Set up a small raised bed garden on supports, so someone confined to a wheelchair can get close enough to enjoy growing and harvesting herbs, vegetables, and flowers.
- Stack cinder building blocks atop one another, offset so their holes are open and free, to quick and inexpensively create a "stackable" garden.
- Plant lettuces, cascading tomatoes, and herbs in hanging baskets and window boxes for easier reach and watering.
- Moving plants indoors and out, or just around and about the garden, is much easier if you have a hand truck with wheels. Its lever action and small wheels makes lifting, turning, and transporting heavy pots more practical. After all, no potted plant is worth a wrenched back!

A Variety of Container Plantings

J ust about anyone can grow something in a pot—from kindergarten kids planting a bean seed in a milk carton, to a garden club matron with blue ribbon orchids, and everything in between. And for the most part, they are all planted and cared for about the same way, with a few twists.

Specialty containers, including window boxes, water gardens, terrariums, and dish gardens, have slight differences in how they are planted, and unusual but easy-to-grow orchids, bonsai, and other attention-grabbing flora are treated a bit differently than more traditional plants.

But it's those variations that spice up the garden, and let everyday gardeners create special planters of favorite plants for that "just right" touch. Whether planting a simple clay pot, an old boot painted purple, a lush hanging basket, or an overstuffed raised bed, the following pages can give a few ideas for some basic types of containers, and a few tricks for getting them started right.

Planting in containers lets you create the look you want.

. . . it's those variations that spice up the garden, and let everyday gardeners create special planters of favorite plants for that "just right" touch.

Now it's up to you to take these standard concepts, experiment with different containers, mix and match plants, and find the perfect spot to display and enjoy your creation.

Planting Supplies Checklist

- Right type and size pot for your plants
- Drain hole cover to keep soil in
- Potting soil for your type of plant
- Shears or knife for cutting tight roots
- Scoop or trowel for potting soil
- Gloves to keep potting soil from drying out your hands
- Fertilizer
- Water
- Odds and ends (stakes, trellis, hanger, plant labels, and so on)

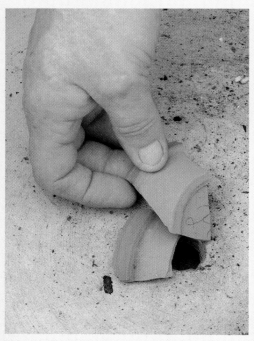

Gardeners have grown individual or groups of plants in single pots since ancient times. Other than variations in modern container materials and new lightweight soilless potting mixes, they have all been done about the same way, by both high-end horticulturists and garden-variety gardeners.

How to do it:

1 Choose the right style and size pot for your plants and garden needs.

2 Cover the drainage hole with a piece of screen or a broken bit of pottery, to keep potting soil from washing out.

Cover the drainage hole.

3 Fill the container partway with slightly moist, prepared potting soil.

4 Place plants in the container, with roots slightly spread out.

Spread the roots as you place plants in the container.

5 Fill in around the plant with more soil, tamping in around roots as you go.

6 Leave an inch or so "head space" between the top of the potting soil and the pot rim to allow for watering.

7 Add a little time-release fertilizer.

8 Water thoroughly twice, to settle soil and remove air pockets from around roots.

Don't forget to fertilize.

Enjoy your work of art.

There is really no need to add a layer of gravel to the bottom of a pot before filling with potting soil; this can actually decrease the amount of air in the soil and increase the amount of water retained. It is best to fill the pot all the way with potting soil, with something over the bottom drainage hole to keep the soil from washing out.

HANGING BASKETS

While hanging baskets can be nearly any size—including half-baskets hung from walls—they are heavy when fully loaded with plants, soil, and water. They also all tend to dry out quickly.

When your sphagnum moss-lined hanging basket is ready to plant, simply plant through the moss.

Most flowers seem to look good together.

Hanging baskets can be preformed plastic, wire lined with moss, or wire with a fitted fiber mat. Moss is attractive but tricky to work with, and has a shorter life than the tightly woven custom-fitted fiber material; however, the more practical fiber mats are quickly covered by plants.

After removing the hangers, plant plastic hanging baskets exactly the same way as regular pots, then re-attach the hangers.

For fiber mat baskets, select a mat that is the right size for your wire basket. Plant exactly as for regular pots, except you can cut small holes in the lower sides and insert small cascading plants.

Hanging baskets are often found near an entryway, where they make visitors feel welcome.

For natural sphagnum moss-lined hanging baskets:

1 Shred and soak the moss in a large bucket of room temperature water for a few minutes.

2 Carefully lay and pack strips of the moist moss, starting from the bottom of the basket, overlapping it so there are no holes for potting soil to wash through.

3 Continue to add potting soil and more plants, exactly as for regular pots.

With garden space and time at a premium, what better way to enjoy growing flowers, herbs, and vegetables than in a large planter box, called a raised bed? Sides can be as high as you need (though the taller the bed, the more water will be needed in the summer), constructed from nearly any kind of sturdy building material—pressure-treated lumber, construction blocks, brick, or concrete are very commonly used—and topped with a surface that can double as seating.

Be sure your raised bed is held together securely.

Build several beds close together if you need more planting space. A bed less than five feet wide will enable you to reach plants in the center.

1 Build your bed the shape and height you want (hint: make it no more than four or five feet across, so you can easily reach plants in the center).

2 Line the inside with heavy gauge plastic (this step is optional).

3 Fill with heavy planter mix that has had topsoil added for firmness.

4 Plant as needed, or even continuously, depending on your climate (raised beds warm early in the spring, and drain well during wet weather).

Raised beds can be used for food or flowers.

Mulches help! Covering your potting soil with a little shredded or chipped bark, gravel, or other loose material will help prevent the soil from "wicking" dry in the sun, at least until the plants have a chance to cover the soil themselves. It can also reduce soil compaction and splashing from watering.

HYPERTUFA STONE TROUGH

You can mix hypertufa yourself.

Make your own hypertufa, or lightweight faux stone, trough using readily available ingredients. It's easy, though time-consuming and a little messy. There are many recipes, all of which more or less work. Here's an easy one:

You will need:

- 2 parts Portland or ready-mix cement
- 1 part coarse or builder's sand
- 2 parts vermiculite, perlite, or peat moss (determines the texture of the end product)
- 1.5 parts water
- Large mixing container
- Cardboard, wood, or plastic box to use as a mold
- Plastic sheeting (split open garbage bag, or use cleaner's plastic)

How to do it:

Mix dry ingredients, then add most of the water, mixing thoroughly to get a stiff mud or clay consistency; gradually add more water as needed to get the consistency you want.

You will probably have to check the consistency by hand.

2 Cover the mold (inside or out, depending on which way you use it) with plastic sheeting to make removal easier later. Then either pack the wet mix tightly inside the mold, starting with a two-inch layer on the bottom and working up the inside, or turn the mold upside down and pack the dough all the way around the outside, at least one inch thick.

3 Poke drainage holes in the bottom before it hardens, or insert small rolled cardboard "sticks" that can be removed later.

4 Cover the container overnight with plastic sheeting to keep it moist.

5 Remove the form, and lightly scour the outside with a metal brush to get an interesting textured surface.

6 Let the trough cure a few days until it hardens completely. Stain or paint if desired.

Pack the hypertufa over or inside the mold you've made.

Here's a completed project.

Be sure the tire is soft so it's easy to cut.

This common container, often scorned as "po' folks" or "country," can easily outlast another recycled pot—the half whiskey barrel—by decades. When cut and inverted, it becomes a modern-day folk art classic. Because only the sidewalls are cut, none of the metal in the steel belts is released into the soil.

Simple steps for making a "crowned" tire planter:

1 Choose a car tire that is soft and rounded in the curve where the sidewall meets the tread (press in with your hand or foot; if it presses easily, it will be easy to invert later).

2 Cut only the soft, metal-free sidewall, using a long, sharp knife (draw a pattern with chalk if necessary). Caution: cut away from yourself, to avoid accidents!

3 With the cut side facing away from you, use your knee to push in on the rounded curve, while pulling the cut side back toward you. This may take practice, but can be done easily if you play around until you find the "sweet spot."

Cut only the soft, metal-free sidewall.

You must invert the tire to plant in it.

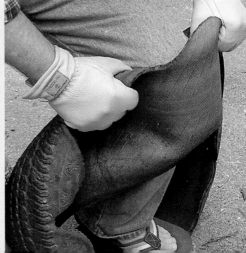

4 With the partly inverted tire flat on the ground, work the rest of the way around the tire pulling as you go.

5 Use a degreaser cleanser to get rid of oily grime before painting with any outdoor paint. Plant as you would any other container.

Some car tires are much easier to invert than others. Step one—finding a good, soft tire—is crucial.

This project is fun for all ages.

A planter made from a recycled tire will far outlast a whiskey barrel, because wood rots.

WINDOW BOX

This classic cottage accessory typically spills with flowers, bulbs, and cascading vines. Little more than a long, narrow box firmly attached to a windowsill or wall, it should be at least eight inches wide and deep, or you will spend all your spare time watering. For a homemade window box, use treated one-inch wood and galvanized or brass screws. Paint or stain it to add to the gaiety. Plant and care is the same as for other containers.

1 Plant in a plastic liner set inside the box to prolong its useful life, or simply set potted plants directly in the box and hide the containers with moss or bark.

2 Fill the window box, and change out seasonally or as needed.

Line the box with plastic or set the potted plants directly in the interior.

You can easily change the plants in a window box.

If you plant annuals in your window box, you can change them to match the season.

STRAWBERRY JAR

Traditional pots with multiple planting holes have long been used for strawberries, small herbs, and other small or cascading plants. They require regular turning to keep all plants equally exposed to the sun. Watering can be a little tricky.

1 Fill the pot with soil up to the first row of holes, and add a little fertilizer.

2 Gently loosen plant roots, and push through the holes, spreading roots out.

3 Fill the pot to the next row of holes, add more fertilizer, and repeat the planting.

4 Insert a plastic watering tube—at least an inch or so in diameter—in the center of the jar, about halfway down inside, for watering the center later.

5 Continue adding soil, fertilizer, and plants, leaving the watering tube in place.

Water the pot from the top and through the planting holes, then fill the water tube with water. It will slowly seep down into the center of the pot to reach more roots.

Don't forget the plastic watering tube—it mal watering easier.

Leave the watering tube in place as you finish the project.

DISH GARDEN

Mismatched teacups look great when filled with similar plants—in this case a variety of succulents.

Shallow saucers, dishes, or large coffee mugs make terrific tabletop conversation pieces, especially for tiny succulents and cacti, miniature herbs, dwarf bulbs, and even moss. They are perfect for children, although they will need help making drainage holes, the most crucial part of the entire project. Plant with a very porous mix, and water often.

Plants need containers that drain, but you can accomplish this with a drill and special masonry bit.

Make a drainage hole using a high-speed electric drill and masonry bit. Take your time, using a steady hand but without applying too much pressure.

Central air conditioning and heating can dry small tropical plants out quickly. Grouping them inside a fish tank (choose a used or inexpensive one) can create the humidity even ferns need for best growth.

1 Line the bottom of a terrarium with pea gravel for drainage.

2 Cover with potting soil, with charcoal dust added to reduce odors.

3 Loosen roots of plants completely, and spread them out over the top of the soil.

4 Add more potting soil over the tops of roots to cover.

5 Keep the terrarium out of direct sunshine, which can cause it to overheat.

6 Water sparingly, and only when the soil gets nearly dry.

7 Prune and thin excess growth of plants as needed to keep them within bounds.

To keep soils from staying soggy and possibly even decaying and beginning to smell, use a large baster to siphon out excess water.

A terrarium retains the humidity most plants need for optimum growth.

HYDROPONICS GARDEN

Rooting plants in water is a time-honored way to keep them over the winter, or to get more to share with friends. Many plants can grow in just water, with a dab of fertilizer added. Change water frequently, to prevent odors.

Rooting plants in water is simple to do and an easy way to increase your supply of plants.

Adding a fish to your hydroponics garden will add interest.

Larger setups are more complicated but still very easy. Most require aeration, which usually involves recirculating pumps and a water/fertilizer reservoir. Easy systems are available, or you can find out how to make your own through research in the library or on the Internet.

PATIO OR DECK WATER GARDEN

With or without an electric water pump, this versatile idea has unlimited possibilities for using small aquatic plants. Special liners are made for half whiskey barrels, or use anything that holds water. Add floating aquatic plants, or pot other water garden plants in clay pots with good topsoil (not potting soil), and raise them near the surface, on bricks.

You may choose to add inexpensive goldfish to your water garden. Realize, however, that even small water gardens can also be home to mosquito larvae. A circulating pump will disturb the water, which prevents mosquitoes from laying eggs. Help avoid an electric shock by always plugging the pump into a ground fault interrupter outlet.

Many water plants are now being offered in miniature forms, including water lilies.

Running water adds to the soothing effect of a water garden, though not all aquatic plants can tolerate it.

Even if your water garden only has one kind of plant in it, it can look beautiful.

BOOT OR SHOE

All ages enjoy this project.

A shoe works just as well as a boot.

There is nothing subtle about this whimsical project, which is simply a variation on planting in a single pot or even a watering can! As long as there is drainage (made by drilling a hole in the sole, if there isn't one already), almost any small plant can be grown in this simple variation of single pot container gardening. Watering regularly will be crucial.

Use low-growing, cascading, or other small plants to prevent the boot from falling over. Instead of planting directly in potting soil in the boot, consider slipping in an already-potted plant.

Who would think that a boot could be a thing of beauty?

WALL CANS

Using the same flower in your wall pots adds to the impact.

Wall pots have a limited amount of dirt, so you'll have to pay more attention to watering and fertilizing.

Whimsy has its place in the garden. These recycled cans are used to create a contemporary recycled effect while toning down a bare garage wall. Brass or galvanized screws are used for attaching directly to the wall. Cans may also be cut down one side, with half the bottom removed, and screwed to a board to be attached to a wall or fence.

Plants should be small, and must tolerate a fair amount of neglect, especially with watering. Slow-release fertilizer makes feeding much less of a chore.

This *Cryptomeria japonica* makes a beautiful bonsai.

There is an astounding array of unusual plants that are surprisingly easy to grow, in spite of having special needs for potting soils, watering, pruning, or environmental adjustments—these plants include orchids, bromeliads, topiary, and bonsai. Master these, and your garden will be vastly more interesting!

As with any unusual topic, there are many books, book chapters, web sites, and local clubs from which you can get ideas, inspiration, and lots of "how-to" tips for these and other specialty plants.

Bonsai is the ancient art of growing miniature shrubs and trees in shallow dishes. Careful trimming of branches, annual root pruning, light feeding, and regular never-miss-a-time watering are crucial for creating and maintaining miniature plants in small containers. Start with small junipers, jade, or other dwarf plants.

Tropical orchids are usually epiphytes, which means they don't need to grow in soil. There are specialty bark mixes and containers specifically for them.

Orchids are perhaps the most exotic plants you can grow. You can choose from several major groups, each with many different types. Some terrestrial ones are grown in regular potting soil, but the most beautiful are the epiphytes, or air plants, that grow in small hanging baskets filled with coarse bark. Orchids require bright, indirect light, high humidity, and regular but very light feedings with liquid plant food.

Bromeliads, either terrestrial or epiphytic, are grown very much like orchids. Pineapple is a popular bromeliad. Most have very colorful leaves, and some have a central cup for holding water. Bromeliads require high humidity, and bright indirect light. Most die after flowering, but produce new plants around their bases.

Topiary is the art of growing tightly pruned evergreen shrubs, and you can mix and match them in ornamental containers for adding either whimsy or classical lines to a patio or deck. They require regular shearing to stay compact.

Water is often captured in the central cup of a bromeliad.

The spiral topiary in this container leads the eye upward along the window.

What's to keep you from having plants that are very pretty, and that you can eat when you get tired of looking at them? Grown exactly like flowers in large containers or raised beds, the best bets are those that are compact and produce a lot over a long time, and are extra colorful or fragrant so they look great up close while they are growing.

This lettuce growing in a tire planter combines two of the projects listed in this chapter: A kitchen garden and planting in an inverted tire.

Try a zesty combination of colorful, nutritious "designer" vegetables; fragrant, flavorful herbs; and even strawberries; dwarf blueberries; and citrus such as kumquat in a mixed collection close to the kitchen where they can be quickly used for more than just good looks.

Like many herbs, rosemary grows well in a container.

Great herbs for containers include rosemary, oregano, chives, garlic chives, mint, cilantro, sage, parsley, and many varieties of basil and thyme.

Tasty vegetables that also look great include Swiss chard, bush and miniature tomatoes, many kinds of peppers, Malabar spinach, eggplant, and a sampler of lettuces.

Easy edible flowers for containers are viola, pansy, rose, squash, nasturtium, rosemary, daylily, chives, and squash.

You can grow your kitchen garden in hanging baskets too, if you wish.

Keep the kitchen garden planted year-round, using hardy perennial herbs as the backbone, and adding interesting kinds of vegetables and even a few edible flowering plants in the appropriate seasons. Harvest and replanting is easy in container gardens!

Vegetables grow well in a raised bed. Add flowers, and you've got something pretty that's also useful.

Can't Miss Container Plant Favorites

Plenty of plants can be grown in containers, and grown well. The only limits are your imagination, available space, and budget! But just because a plant can be confined to a pot doesn't mean it will thrive, look good, or be easy to care for. Some do better than others, so we have assembled some descriptive lists to help you make selections. From annuals to perennials, herbs to flowering bulbs, houseplants to tropical plants to cacti, not to mention a few vines, shrubs, and small trees, there are myriad "can't miss" choices. You are off to a good start in your container-gardening adventures when you pick something from these lists. Have fun!

In this chapter, you will find dozens of helpful profiles, spanning all the categories listed above. Obviously, this is but a sampling of all that the plant world has to offer, but the ones on this list are special. To assure your gardening success, they have been tried and tested, passing muster on the following key criteria:

- attractive flowers
- dependable performance
- easy care
- wide availability

Morning Glory
(Ipomoea purpurea)

AT A GLANCE ICONS

At the bottom of each entry, you will notice small graphic icons. They convey additional useful information about the plant's characteristics or benefits.

attracts butterflies		native plant	
attracts hummingbirds		supports bees	
produces edible fruit		wildlife plant	
has fragrance		good fall color	
produces attractive fruit		drought resistant	
suitable for cut flowers		award winner	
long bloom period			

full sun		part shade
part sun		full shade

Winning Plants

In some of these entries, you will learn that a certain plant or a particular selection of it has won an award. This is a great place to start your hunt for the best of the best.

AAS: All-America Selections

Commonly awarded to annuals (and vegetable varieties), this honor is bestowed on an elite group of plants each year. They were grown in trial gardens nationwide and evaluated by experts, usually beating out lots of competitors. The award signals that a plant has not only been judged excellent in the context of its peers, but is widely adaptable.

To learn more, visit the website at www.all-americaselections.org.

**Asparagus Fern
(Asparagus densiflorus)**

PPA: Perennial Plant Association

Only one plant wins Plant of the Year annually, after being nominated and winning the most votes from a group of experts. Who are those experts? Members of the association are nursery owners and staffers, growers and hybridizers, including all sorts of professionals who develop, raise, and market perennials to the American public. They know their plants!

To learn more, visit the website at www.perennialplant.org.

Key to Botanical Terms

Some of these entries include terms that may be unfamiliar to you, but are in common use not only in gardening books but on nursery tags and in plant-catalog descriptions as well. Here's what they mean:

Bract: a showy leaf at the base of a flower or group of flowers, not always green.

Corm: not actually a bulb, although it resembles one; modified stem tissue that remains underground, storing energy for the plant above.

Cultivar: literally short for "cultivated variety," it refers to a plant that was selected for desirable characteristics such as flower color, bloom size, or attractive, distinctive foliage. The plant was given its own, often descriptive name, and will maintain its uniqueness when propagated (reproduced sexually or asexually).

Deadhead: the practice of removing spent flowers. This prevents a plant's natural tendency to begin going to seed or forming fruit. A deadheaded plant tends to redirect that energy into producing still more flowers!

Disk flowers: this is the center, or cone, of daisies and similar flowers. Disk flowers are actually a compact group of small, tube-shaped flowers.

Flower head: a cluster or group of small flowers that at a glance or from a distance look like one bigger flower.

Palmate: Leaves that are shaped like the palm of a hand—fanlike from a common point.

Panicle: a group of flowers arranged on a branched stem.

Silver Dollar Vine
(Dichondra repens)

Raceme: a group of flowers arranged on a central, or single, stalk; the youngest flowers are at the tip.

Ray flowers: on daisies and related plants, these are usually thought of as the petals, or outer petals.

Rhizome: swollen, moisture-retaining, creeping underground stem.

Spathe: a bract or leaf enveloping a subtended flower cluster.

Tuber: it looks a bit like an odd-shaped (not round) or small bulb, but is actually a swollen, underground stem modified to store food energy for the plant.

Umbel: a flower cluster that is either globe shaped or flat topped, but is composed of florets arranged on short little stalks emanating from a single central point.

Annuals

annuals always have been and always will be favorites for containers of all kinds, from small pots to extensive planter boxes to everything in between. This is because annuals are built for temporary and colorful displays—and they deliver. Indeed, the very definition of an annual is a plant that goes from seed to maturity in just one season, a truly remarkable performance when you come to think of it. So gardeners keep turning to annuals.

When you grow an annual in the confined space of a pot, you have full control over the effect. You can choose the plant, the flower color, and the leaf color; you can pick a simpatico pot; and you can place the duo anywhere you want. You can move it later if you want. You can combine several annuals for a fuller, more diverse display. You can yank out and replace any plant that disappoints you or turns out not to suit your purposes.

For that brief but glorious window of summertime color, annuals are simply unbeatable. You can't miss with the ones described below, but you should also range further afield into our "Other Annuals to Try" list or spend extra time down at your local nursery, sniffing out good ones that are new to you. After all, a reliable and enthusiastic annual in any sort of container is a guaranteed good show!

Angelonia
Angelonia angustifolia
MATURE HEIGHT × WIDTH: 12 inches × 12 inches
FLOWER COLORS: violet, purple, pink, bicolors
FLOWER SIZE: racemes of up to 8 inches
BLOOM TIME: summer
SOIL: moist, well drained

Characterized by one horticulturist as "snapdragons on steroids," angelonia is a relatively new sight at garden centers and is certainly a step up from that old standby. Originally hailing from tropical and subtropical Central and South America, this handsome plant prospers in a container. Its habit is bushy and upright. The plants do resemble snapdragons a bit, but the rich flower colors and excellent basal branching make them more desirable to some gardeners. Overall, they are more tidy and formal in appearance than most snapdragons.

Angelonia thrives in warm conditions and a well-drained, fertile soil mix. For most of the summer, its stems are adorned with those unique flowers. It fits in easily to mixed pots of other flowering annuals, though a solo display is also very appealing.

GOOD CHOICES: Deep plum 'Carita'; 'Angel Mist' mix

Coleus
Solenostemon scutellarioides and hybrids
MATURE HEIGHT × WIDTH: 1-3 feet × 1-3 feet
FLOWER COLORS: shades of purple
FLOWER SIZE: small spikes
BLOOM TIME: summer
SOIL: average, well drained

Coleus once was so widely grown that people just got tired of it. Easy to grow and generally untroubled by any pests or diseases, true. Always easy in pots, asking little more than regular watering. But also, frankly, dull.

At some point, horticulturists rediscovered this good old stalwart and started generating all sorts of new varieties. Coleus plants tend to be raised from cuttings, which makes distributing newcomers far and wide a simple matter. Nowadays, the number of variations—and the undeniable beauty of these variations—is astonishing.

For those container gardeners who consider coleus a supporting player, many of the nifty recent introductions are tempting indeed. So intriguing are some of the newest ones, however, that you may just decide to display them solo in a pot—and prominently, for all to admire.

GOOD CHOICES: The exciting new Kong Series has large, dramatic leaves—look for 'Kong Mosaic', or 'Kong Rose', and 'Black Dragon'.

Fan Flower
Scaevola aemula
MATURE HEIGHT × WIDTH: 6-24 inches × 4 feet
FLOWER COLORS: lilac, purple, white
FLOWER SIZE: $1/2$-1 inch
BLOOM TIME: summer
SOIL: average to moist, well drained

Because of its bushy, somewhat trailing habit, fan flower is outstanding in a hanging basket or spilling over the sides of a pot. The dainty flowers are plentiful, and present for most of the summer. The plant is at its best in an average soil mix in a spot in full or dappled sunshine. Although it is a fairly tough customer, you shouldn't let it dry out: Regular, thorough waterings are best. If you don't want to grow it in a basket, try it in a window box or as part of a mixed display in a larger pot. In any event, expect to get plenty of color for very little effort.

Its botanical name comes from the Latin *scaeva*, which means "left-handed"—which refers to the unique hand- or fan-shaped form of the small flowers. Traditionally found in blue, lilac-blue, and purple, fan flower is now also seen in pink and white. Mixing several hues together can make a fine display.

GOOD CHOICES: 'Blue Wonder' is the best, nonfading blue.

Geranium
Pelargonium × hortorum
MATURE HEIGHT × WIDTH: 1-2 feet × 1-2 feet
FLOWER COLORS: red, orange, pink, white
FLOWER SIZE: 3- to 5-inch clusters
BLOOM TIME: summer
SOIL: moist, well drained

This group deserves a fresh look! Even the overused red-flowered geraniums have seen significant improvements in recent years. Nowadays you can expect beautiful, dense flower clusters, attractively patterned leaves, and longer bloom periods. The blossom colors are of much better quality too— there are clear, unmuddied scarlet; the most refreshing whites; and even orange, just to name a few. Last but not least, of special interest to container gardeners, the newer crop of geraniums has denser, much less lanky growth habits.

To look their best, you must provide your geraniums with good, well-drained soil and a little attention from time to time. This means regular watering during dry spells, snipping off blemished or dried-up leaves, and pinching back excessive growth. In return, they will surely look fabulous. Display one to a pot—perhaps in an imposing urn, or fill a sunny window box with several plants, with confidence.

GOOD CHOICES: 2002 AAS winner 'Black Velvet Rose' has pure pink flowers and nearly black leaves; burgundy-red 'Merlot'; pastel-hued 'Summer Showers Mix'.

Impatiens
Impatiens walleriana
MATURE HEIGHT × WIDTH: 6-24 inches × 1-2 feet
FLOWER COLORS: pastels, white, red, orange-red
FLOWER SIZE: 1-2^1/$_2$ inches
BLOOM TIME: summer
SOIL: moist, well drained

You can bring color to dim or shady spots in your yard by placing pots of flowers there. Of course, you need something that will actually bloom in shade, and for that, impatiens is always a fine choice. Indeed, you can count on the plants to remain in bloom for many long weeks. (For bright and sunny patios and decks, the vivacious, bright-colored New Guinea hybrids are outstanding.)

Although this plant has been around for a long time, the newer varieties are clearly superior in terms of uniform flower color, flower size, and a tidier growth habit. For best results, make sure the soil doesn't dry out. Garden centers and seed companies offer a great range of hues. Buy or raise a mixed flat and have fun distributing the plants by twos and threes in pots, or filling window boxes or planter boxes with a rainbow of color.

GOOD CHOICES: There are dozens! Some are single-flowered, some double; the New Guinea ones tolerate sun better; the "African" ones extend the color range to yellow.

Licorice Plant
Helichrysum petiolare
MATURE HEIGHT × WIDTH: 1^1/$_2$-2 feet × 1^1/$_2$-2 feet
FLOWER COLORS: cream
FLOWER SIZE: tiny
BLOOM TIME: summer to fall
SOIL: average, well drained

Abundant, pretty, heart-shaped leaves are the attraction of this plant. Their texture is soft and woolly, which adds to their appeal. (Very small flowers do appear, but are best pinched off so they don't detract from the foliage.) The stems are naturally trailing, so licorice plant is excellent in mixed containers where it can spill over the sides. Its soft color and texture are always welcome and never compete.

Because this plant is so agreeable, you can do a lot of different things with it. Its soft hue is stunning as a foil for rich magenta petunias. Paired with feverfew, its more romantic nature comes out and the display looks like a cottage garden vignette in miniature. Where other plants tower over it, licorice plant obligingly fills in a carpet at their feet.

The plant's only drawback is its susceptibility to insect pests. Keep air circulation good by not crowding it, and don't overwater.

GOOD CHOICES: The leaves of 'Limelight' are chartreuse, while those of 'Variegatum' feature attractive cream markings.

Melampodium
Melampodium paludosum
MATURE HEIGHT × WIDTH: 8-12 inches × 8-12 inches
FLOWER COLORS: yellow
FLOWER SIZE: 1-2 inches
BLOOM TIME: summer
SOIL: average, well drained

An easygoing daisy-laden plant, melampodium is destined for wide popularity (though it could use a sporty, widely accepted common name!). It forms low, bushy mounds that are dense with handsome gray-green leaves and studded with little golden blossoms. It fills a pot all by itself, but also contributes plentiful, foolproof color to larger mixed containers.

The flower show goes on all summer long, with minimal assistance from you—once established, the plants are quite drought- and heat tolerant. In mild climates, expect a year-round show, especially if you remember to keep the container watered and pinch off spent blossoms to encourage re-bloom. Note, however, that this plant also tolerates cool weather well, so gardeners in northern climates can enjoy its little daisies. In any event, melampodium is certainly a great way to get lots of perky, summer-long color for very little effort.

GOOD CHOICES: 'Derby' requires no deadheading.

Nasturtium
Tropaeolum majus
MATURE HEIGHT × WIDTH: 8-15 inches × 12-15 inches
FLOWER COLORS: orange, yellow, red, white
FLOWER SIZE: 2-3 inches
BLOOM TIME: summer
SOIL: well drained

Nasturtiums are a splendid choice for containers. They grow eagerly from seed or from small plants, and they are always generous with their brightly hued flowers. Both bushy and trailing varieties are available and grow in almost any sunny spot. Traditionally orange or yellow, there are now crimson ones, cream-colored ones, lemon-yellow ones, and varieties with dappled leaves for extra impact.

The plants have a pleasant peppery smell and all plant parts are completely edible. The leaves can be used in salads; the flowers are a pretty and tasty garnish. Even the seedpods can be added to summer recipes.

Nasturtiums want only sunshine and regular water. Use them in pots or in hanging baskets, alone or tucked in at the feet of taller flowers. Climbing and trailing ones can be trained to cascade down a rock wall or up over a trellis.

GOOD CHOICES: The Alaska mix has lovely variegated leaves; the Jewel mix has flowers in hot colors; 'Peach Melba' is a vanilla-white flower with maroon markings.

Pansy
Viola × wittrockiana

MATURE HEIGHT × WIDTH: 6-9 inches × 6-9 inches
FLOWER COLORS: many
FLOWER SIZE: 2¹/₂-4 inches
BLOOM TIME: spring into summer
SOIL: moist, well drained

Merry little blossoms abound on these utterly dependable old favorites. Some have a splash of contrasting yellow in the centers, some have blotchy markings called "faces," and still others have "whiskers" radiating from the centers—but all are pretty and durable flowers. The hybridizers have thoroughly explored and expanded the color range, so you can now get a pansy in almost any hue you want. Some are dark and velvety, others are bright and bold, and still others are lovely pastel shades.

Pansies are excellent in containers. They look best in small, unified doses (mix-and-match displays run the risk of looking too busy). Alternatively, add a skirt of pansies at the base of other taller plants, in a color-compatible hue. They also mix very well with foliage plants such as ivy and helichrysum, displays where they are the main source of color. In any event, these endearing flowers prefer some shade, and the pots will require extra water during very hot summer weather.

GOOD CHOICES: 'Purple Rain'; 'Antique Shades'; 'Padparadja'; 'Rhapsody Mix'—gorgeous!

Persian Shield
Strobilanthes dyerianus

MATURE HEIGHT × WIDTH: 2-4 feet × 2-4 feet
FLOWER COLORS: lilac
FLOWER SIZE: 1¹/₂ inch
BLOOM TIME: late summer-fall
SOIL: rich, well drained

Hot, humid summers? This will be a good plant for your pot displays, as it can take the heat. Technically, it's a very tender perennial, but it's always grown as an annual—partly because it's not at all cold hardy, but also because carried-over plants develop woody stems and their leaves are just not as nice as young, fresh ones.

This plant is prized for its bold ornamental foliage. It's undeniably gorgeous, dark lustrous green flushed with purple and dusted with a silvery sheen on top and all purple underneath. The overall effect tends to be purple, which is why this is a popular pot plant—the color is versatile. It looks great with bright-hued flowering annuals, particularly impatiens, vinca, and pentas.

Which brings us to yet another plus about this plant—it tolerates shade well, which means you can tuck some color into spots that need it. Persian shield will grow fine in limited light.

GOOD CHOICES: There are no cultivars. Related *S. atropurpureus* has better flowers and is much more cold hardy.

Petunia
Petunia × hybrida
MATURE HEIGHT × WIDTH: 12-14 inches × up to 3 feet
FLOWER COLORS: many
FLOWER SIZE: up to 4 inches
BLOOM TIME: summer
SOIL: moist, well drained

For sheer dependability, petunias are hard to beat as pot plants. They've been around, and valued, for what seems like ages, but have enjoyed a recent flurry of attention and awards. The colors of the larger, frilly-flowered ones have improved, and the petals are tougher. For the smaller-flowered, trailing ones, the "Wave" petunias have been a revolution, so productive and tough and beautiful are they.

Old-fashioned favorites or highly touted new introductions, petunias still require good soil that drains well (so you cannot skip drainage holes in their containers). Avoid placing the pots in exposed locations where hot sun blasts the life out of them and wind or rain tatters the flower petals. Get down to the garden center in early spring for the best array of choices, or check out the tantalizing selections in mail-order catalogs and order early.

GOOD CHOICES: 2004 AAS winner 'Limbo Violet'; 2003 AAS winners 'Merlin Blue Morn' and 'Blue Wave'; 2002 AAS winner 'Lavender Wave' and 1994 AAS winner 'Purple Wave'.

Silver Dollar Plant
Dichondra micrantha
MATURE HEIGHT × WIDTH: 12-20 inches × sprawling
FLOWER COLORS: pale yellow, pale green, white
FLOWER SIZE: tiny
BLOOM TIME: summer to fall
SOIL: fertile, well drained

This plant has something of an "Ugly Duckling" story. Because it grows vigorously and has nice, trailing stems that root by surface runners, it debuted as a groundcover or grass substitute. But it had some liabilities: It couldn't tolerate foot traffic very well, it wasn't all that cold hardy, and flea beetles nibbled it. However, it was wonderfully heat tolerant.

Then some enterprising gardener or horticulturist somewhere recognized its potential as a container-grown plant, and that is where we find it today. The trailing habit is indeed a virtue, as the plant fills in and cascades over a window box, planter box, or hanging basket appealingly. And the color has turned out to be another plus. The most widely available pest-resistant form is called 'Silver Falls', which forms a mass of fan-shaped, shimmery silver leaves. It goes great with fiery colors but also flatters pastels. Try it with one of the Wave petunias or angelonia. For an all-foliage display, try it with chartreuse sweet potato vine or coleus.

GOOD CHOICES: 'Silver Falls' and 'Emerald Falls'.

Star Clusters
Pentas lanceolata
MATURE HEIGHT × WIDTH: 1-2 feet × 1-2 feet
FLOWER COLORS: shades of pink, red, purple, white
FLOWER SIZE: 3- to 4-inch clusters
BLOOM TIME: summer
SOIL: fertile, well drained

Technically a tender tropical shrubby plant, this performs beautifully in most of North America as an exuberant summertime pot-grown annual. The crisp green foliage serves as a handsome backdrop for lots of perky flower clusters that give the plant its common name. It's especially long-blooming, which is a big plus when you are looking for reliable color.

Though usually available in mixes, you can also get star clusters in individual colors or white, which helps if you have a special color theme in mind or are making a hanging basket display. Butterflies and hummingbirds flock to the flowers if you place the container where they can reach it.

Site containers of star clusters in full sun, and remember to water and fertilize regularly so the plant will look its very best. If you snip the flowers to add to bouquets, you'll appreciate the fact that they are especially long lasting.

GOOD CHOICES: Garden Sparkles mix has dense clusters in the white-pink-red range; 'Star White' is the finest all-white one.

Swedish Ivy
Plectranthus species and cultivars
MATURE HEIGHT × WIDTH: 1-3 feet × 1-3 feet
FLOWER COLORS: pink, mauve, white, lilac
FLOWER SIZE: 1/2 inch
BLOOM TIME: summer
SOIL: well drained

Valuable for adding foliage interest to summer pot displays, Swedish ivy plants come in a variety of leaf hues and forms. The classic houseplant one with the scalloped leaves is *Plectranthus australis*, but other species and hybrids have heart-shaped foliage; some have white rims on each leaf, some have pinkish stems. They are usually aromatic, for this genus is in the mint family. (If it should flower, which it doesn't always, you'll see the mint resemblance right away—perky, erect little clusters of two-lipped flowers.)

There's another mint-family characteristic: it grows fast. So to keep your Swedish ivy in bounds in the container you have chosen for it, you will have to intervene and pinch back stems regularly. In response, the plant will grow denser and bushier. If you forget, you can trim back too-long or lanky growth and the plant will recover and generate new leaves easily.

GOOD CHOICES: The relatively recent hybrid 'Mona Lavender' is a beauty.

Twinspur
Diascia barberae and hybrids
MATURE HEIGHT × WIDTH: 10 inches × 20 inches
FLOWER COLORS: pink, rose, red
FLOWER SIZE: ¹/₂-³/₄ inch
BLOOM TIME: summer
SOIL: moist, well drained

A relative newcomer, twinspur is related to snapdragons, and this is apparent in the tubular, lobed flowers. However, it is a lower-growing, mat-forming plant with slender, graceful stems bearing the unique and beautiful blooms. Twinspur is able to both fill in and spill over a bit, making it well suited to window boxes and pots. Grow it alone to call attention to the pretty flowers (or combine different flower colors—it comes in various shades of pink, rosy pink, and ruby red). Added to a container of various other plants, it will be dependable and yet not steal the spotlight.

Please note that especially hot weather is not good for twinspur plants, but otherwise they are a cinch to grow well. All they ask is a spot in ample sunlight and fertile, well-drained, evenly moist soil. To keep them in constant bloom, just snip back spent flowers and wait for more.

GOOD CHOICES: 'Ruby Field' is widely acknowledged as the best bright pink; 'Blackthorn Apricot', from England, is a lovely, softer shade of apricot-pink.

Verbena
Verbena × hybrida (V. × hortensis)
MATURE HEIGHT × WIDTH: 1-2 feet × 1-2 feet
FLOWER COLORS: purple to red, white
FLOWER SIZE: 3-inch clusters
BLOOM TIME: summer
SOIL: average, well drained

A favorite heat-loving annual, common verbena is wonderfully dependable. The foliage is generally a nice, neat green, and the flower clusters—mostly in shades of purple and red, often with contrasting white eyes—are plentiful. Some have a sweet scent, and hummingbirds and butterflies are drawn to them. You can also clip the flowers to add to mixed bouquets. Verbena is color you can count on.

You often see verbena in hanging baskets or sprawling over the lip of urns. But don't overlook mixed-container possibilities. Verbena is very nice with other sun-lovers, from dramatic, fan-shaped yuccas to lamb's ears (*Stachys*).

Growth will be bushier and more compact if you pinch it back occasionally. It is a sun-lover that tolerates dry weather well, but pots can dry out in those conditions and the plants will eventually show their distress. It's wise to give them an occasional good soaking.

GOOD CHOICES: 'Quartz Burgundy' was an AAS winner in 1999; 'Tickled Pink'; the Romance series.

Other annuals to try in containers:

- **Chenille Plant,** *Acalypha hispida*
- **Creeping Zinnia,** *Sanvitalia procumbens* cultivars (top left)
- **Dusty Miller,** *Senecio cineraria*
- **Flowering Tobacco,** *Nicotiana alata* cultivars
- **Heliotrope,** *Heliotropium arborescens*
- **Joseph's Coat,** *Alternanthera ficoidea*

- **Lobelia, Edging,** *Lobelia erinus*
- **Moss Rose,** *Portulaca grandiflora* (top right)
- **Mum,** *Chrysanthemum* or *Dendranthema* cultivars
- **Primrose,** *Primula × polyantha*
- **Scarlet Sage,** *Salvia splendens* (center)
- **Zinnia, Dwarf,** *Zinnia* species and cultivars (Profusion Series, *Z. angustifolius*)

Bulbs, Corms, and Tubers

If you've grown bulbs only in the ground, raising them in containers will give you a whole new appreciation! You'll now get to enjoy small ones, those with small flowers, and those with fragrance up close. With larger plants, pot culture lets you grow them well and display them closer to where you can see them daily. And because many of these plants are not cold hardy, raising them in pots lets you grow them wherever you live.

Growing bulbs in pots gives you control over your displays. Bring them out when they are looking their best or about to flower, and move them to a holding area or even discard them when they start to flag.

When to plant depends on the sort of bulb. Tender or tropical bulbs should be potted in warm weather. Spring-flowering favorites are planted in the fall. Bulbs should not be allowed to freeze, and potted ones will be vulnerable if your winters are quite cold. In this case, shelter your potted bulbs in a garage, perhaps, or in a breezeway or a cold frame. If your winters are mild, you need to either buy bulbs specifically labeled "pre-chilled," or refrigerate before planting them.

Remember that your bulbs depend on your vigilant care to thrive. Bulbs consume plenty of water, especially in warm weather. Nutrients that were present in the soil mix when you potted up your beauties tend to leach away, so you should combine plant food with your water deliveries.

When colder weather comes, you have some choices. You can discard your potted bulbs, shake them out of the pot and put them in the ground, or sink the entire pot into the ground (a protective mulch may be in order). Or you can bring them indoors to a cool spot, reduce water and fertilizer, and allow them to wait in a dormant, or at least slowed-down, state.

Agapanthus
Agapanthus species and cultivars
MATURE HEIGHT × WIDTH: 2¹/₂-4 feet × 2 feet
FLOWER COLORS: blue, white, pink
FLOWER SIZE: 5- to 8-inch flower heads
BLOOM TIME: summer to early fall
SOIL: average, well drained
ZONES: 8-10

In mild-climate areas of California, especially, the strappy leaves and big lollipop flowers of sun-loving agapanthus are a common sight—even neglected and dusty in parking lot planter boxes and curbside plantings.

It's easy to grow agapanthus in a container, although one with some heft and depth is obviously advisable. Plunked in the middle, in a well-drained mix of average fertility, the plant will first generate straplike leaves. The clump is nicely symmetrical in a round pot, tub, or urn, and when the bare stalks arise from the middle, the display is all the more satisfying.

Although loose, lilac-blue flower heads are the most common, look into some of the new and improved cultivars and colors. There are denser ones, as well as white, pink, and darker blue choices. You can also expect more than one flower stalk per plant from the newcomers.

GOOD CHOICES: The Headbourne Hybrids; 'Prolific Blue' and 'Prolific White'.

Amaryllis
Hippeastrum cultivars
MATURE HEIGHT × WIDTH: 18-24 inches × 8-12 inches
FLOWER COLORS: red, pink, white, yellow, green
FLOWER SIZE: up to 8 inches across
BLOOM TIME: fall and winter
SOIL: average, well drained
ZONES: 10-11

"Just add water and stand back!" trumpets the bulb catalog. Are amaryllis really that easy to grow? In a word: yes—at least if you start with good quality, healthy, plump bulbs.

Every fall and winter, you can buy "amaryllis kits" for holiday displays. If you want to save money, or have a pot on hand for an amaryllis, purchase the bulb alone. Just be sure that your pot is able to bear the weight and height of the coming show. Pot the roundish bulb into the growing medium with its "nose and shoulders" aboveground. Then just add water and stand back.

The trend is toward bigger individual blooms and multiple blooms, but the strappy leaves and flower stalks seem to be short, which makes for top-heavy plants. If you find these "convenient" amaryllis mutant-looking, return to the good old towering plants of old and support your blossoms with simple wire stakes.

GOOD CHOICES: Huge-flowered, productive 'Grand Trumpet'; a taller, older variety is pink 'Appleblossom'.

Begonia, Tuberous
Begonia × tuberhybrida
MATURE HEIGHT × WIDTH: 8-12 inches × 8-12 inches
FLOWER COLORS: many
FLOWER SIZE: 4-6 inches
BLOOM TIME: summer to fall
SOIL: average, well drained
ZONES: 10-11

For splashy, long-lasting color in partially or fully shady areas, tuberous begonias are without peer. Grow them in pots, window boxes, or hanging baskets, in a well-drained mix, with the fat tubers placed only about an inch deep. If you put more than one to a container, space them about 6 inches apart so they have enough elbow room.

Growth can be slow at first, but when the first blooms burst on the scene, all is forgiven! They are big, often fluffy, and abounding in confident, bold color (technically, what you are admiring are the male flowers; the female flowers are smaller and single).

Tuberous begonias remain in constant bloom all summer, only slowing or halting when fall frosts threaten. Water regularly to keep the soil moist, and water at the roots so the leaves don't get damp.

GOOD CHOICES: There are dozens of varieties. Choose by sub-type (camellia-flowered, non-stop, picotee, cascade, or lace) and then select your colors.

Caladium
Caladium bicolor, hybrids
MATURE HEIGHT × WIDTH: 1-2 feet × 1-2 feet
FLOWER COLORS: greenish-white spathes
FLOWER SIZE: up to 9 inches high
BLOOM TIME: spring
SOIL: rich, well drained
ZONES: 9-10

Here is one of the most valuable, lush-growing foliage plants for shade. It's super-easy to grow, asking only for a fertile growing medium. The more humusy, the better, actually, especially in areas with very hot summers where the plants might otherwise dry out quickly. The pot needs a drainage hole, and you should keep the medium moist but never soggy. That's it!

Each plant grows from a small, chubby tuber, from which the broadly heart-shaped leaves emerge on short stalks. Containers of mix-and-match displays look terrific, but if you get carried away with too many different kinds the pots can look "too busy." Single pots of a single variety are always nice, or you can grow one with a color-complementary companion, such as a white tuberous begonia with a backdrop of a white-and-green-leaved caladium.

GOOD CHOICES: There are hundreds of named varieties; your best bet is to carefully peruse the color and pattern choices.

Canna
Canna species and hybrids
MATURE HEIGHT × WIDTH: 4-8 feet × 1-2 feet
FLOWER COLORS: red, yellow, orange, pink, multi
FLOWER SIZE: 2-3 inches
BLOOM TIME: summer
SOIL: fertile, well drained
ZONES: 8-11

Hot color! Rely on potted cannas to supply plentiful and fiery color in your summer container displays. Blooming is from midsummer until fall. While the big, paddle-shaped leaves are often dark green (a great backdrop for those vivid flowers), some cannas feature yellow-striped leaves that can steal the show. Burgundy-foliaged ones are also quite stunning.

Cannas are also tall, stately plants, so they need substantial pots or they'll topple over. Some gardeners like to cluster pots together in a sunny spot, such as a corner of a deck, at an entryway, or by the pool. Individual pots may also be tucked into a regular flower border for an unexpected punch of tropical pizzazz.

Whatever you decide, it's important to take care of your potted cannas so they'll look fantastic. This begins with the potting medium, which must be light but fertile. Consistent water is key; if the rhizomes dry out, the whole display falters.

GOOD CHOICES: 'Pretoria' (also sold as 'Bengal Tiger'); 'Rosemond Cole'; 'Tropical Rose'.

Daffodil
Narcissus species and cultivars
MATURE HEIGHT × WIDTH: 6-18 inches × 6-12 inches
FLOWER COLORS: white or yellow
FLOWER SIZE: 2-5 inches
BLOOM TIME: spring
SOIL: fertile, well drained
ZONES: 3-8

Salute spring with pretty pots of daffodils. As in the ground, place the bulbs pointy end up and about twice as deep as the bulb is tall. They will be well anchored, plus their roots can be accommodated in the lower part of the pot. Regular potting mixes are a bit too light for them; mix in some organic matter to make the medium more substantial.

For smaller containers, more compact varieties are appropriate. Otherwise, any daffodil you want may be grown in a larger pot, tub, or half-barrel. Single-color or single-variety displays can be sensational. Otherwise, feel free to include daffodils in mixed-bulb container shows, where their generally yellow or white flowers inject freshness into groupings of red, purple, orange, or pink flowers.

Daffodils don't tend to last another year in the pot; so you're best off considering the show a one-time event.

GOOD CHOICES: Cyclamineus (showy, flared blooms) and triandrus (with multiple fragrant flowers).

Dahlia
Dahlia cultivars, dwarf types
MATURE HEIGHT × WIDTH: 8-15 inches × 8-15 inches
FLOWER COLORS: many, including bicolors
FLOWER SIZE: 2-4 inches for dwarfs
BLOOM TIME: late summer into fall
SOIL: average, well drained
ZONES: 8-10

The smaller-flowered, smaller-size dahlias are superb for pots, window boxes, tubs, and other containers. They come in the same vibrant colors as their "dinner-plate-size" flowered kin, including spunky bicolors, though they are much smaller. (Merchants loosely use many categories to promote these, including "border dahlias," "patio dahlias," and "pompon dahlias.") But they grow from the same sort of fat tuberous roots, have the same type of foliage, and make it well into fall.

For best results, pot yours in a light mix that holds moisture well (with some peat content). Too much moisture causes the clumping roots to rot, so be sure the container has drainage holes and be careful not to overwater. Plant the clumps in late spring, about 4 inches down. Once the plants are up and growing, in early summer, you may pinch back growing tips to encourage more compact growth. Boost flowering with occasional doses of a balanced fertilizer.

GOOD CHOICES: Look for border, patio, or pompon varieties; 'Bishop's Children' is a vivid mix.

Freesia
Freesia cultivars
MATURE HEIGHT × WIDTH: 8-10 inches × 2-4 inches
FLOWER COLORS: white, cream, yellow, pink, red, violet
FLOWER SIZE: 1- to 3-inch trumpets
BLOOM TIME: spring
SOIL: light, well drained
ZONES: 9-11

Though they seem rather delicate, with their exquisite blossoms and fragrance, freesias are not tricky to grow. The only hitch is your patience—they take up to four months to start producing flowers. Because they're not at all cold hardy, the obvious solution is to raise them in pots.

Freesias grow from small corms, planted three or five to a pot, about an inch deep. Use a light mix, with some sand or airy peat moss mixed in. Keep them warm and well watered, and the foliage will arrive and eventually the enchanting flowers. If the stems become floppy, rig supports with slender sticks and green string.

Show off your potted freesias at eye level, so you and visitors can savor their beauty and that heady scent. The flowers may last for up to a month if you're lucky!

When to plant freesias—and thus when to enjoy them—depends on planning around that long lead-up.

GOOD CHOICES: Available as "singles" or "doubles"; the singles seem more fragrant, but the doubles are more showy.

Grape Hyacinth

Muscari armeniacum, M. azureum

MATURE HEIGHT × WIDTH: 6-8 inches × 6-8 inches
FLOWER COLORS: blue, white
FLOWER SIZE: 1- to 3-inch spikes
BLOOM TIME: spring
SOIL: average, well drained
ZONES: 4-7

Often taken for granted out in the garden proper, pot-raised grape hyacinths are a real delight. Their spiky form and chubby little bells of cobalt blue or white stand out from the crowd, especially if you devote an entire pot to a display of nothing else. Mixing some blue- and white-flowered ones together also makes a thrilling show. Use a decorative pot for even more impact. The foliage, which is grassy and green, never detracts.

Pot-grown grape hyacinths are also fine companions. Blue pansies are quite pretty with them, as are contrasting-hued yellow pansies. Or you could combine them with the much bigger hyacinths; so the display doesn't look skimpy, plant more grape hyacinths.

The bulbs are small and fleshy and tend to dry out quickly, so start out with fresh ones and to plant promptly. Use an average, well-draining potting mix, place the pots in a spot in full or partial sun, and water regularly.

GOOD CHOICES: 'Blue Spike' has the best blue flowers; 'Album' is a crisp white.

Hyacinth

Hyacinthus orientalis

MATURE HEIGHT × WIDTH: 8-10 inches × 6-8 inches
FLOWER COLORS: blue, purple, red, pink, yellow, white
FLOWER SIZE: 6- to 8-inch spikes
BLOOM TIME: early to mid-spring
SOIL: fertile, well drained
ZONES: 5-9

The big draw for these springtime favorites is their luxurious perfume. The color is also appealing, especially because you can now get hyacinths in every hue of blue and purple imaginable. There are also soft pinks, rosy pinks, soft yellows, and pure whites. The "double" ones are fuller, because each floret has a second floret blooming in its center.

Hyacinths seem to have a formal air, which sometimes makes them difficult to place out in the garden proper. The solution is to display your hyacinths in pots and position them strategically where their formal beauty is an asset—along a deck or marching up a walkway or stairs, or arrayed in a window box.

For best results, plant your hyacinth bulbs deeply in pots of well-drained mix in the fall, so they can start forming roots. Keep them from freezing over the winter.

GOOD CHOICES: White 'Carnegie'; yellow 'City of Haarlem'; ruby red 'Jan Bos'; dark blue 'Blue Jacket'.

Lily
Lilium cultivars (dwarfs)
MATURE HEIGHT × WIDTH: 18-36 inches × 12 inches
FLOWER COLORS: many
FLOWER SIZE: 4-7 inches
BLOOM TIME: summer, varies
SOIL: fertile, well drained
ZONES: 5-9 for most

Majestic lilies are truly one of the most gorgeous flowers one can grow, and well within the reach of container gardeners. You just have to choose wisely. Go for shorter or "dwarf" lilies, and choose a substantial container.

There are different kinds of lilies. The ones you see most often—listed here in order of bloom time, starting in early summer into late summer—are Asiatics, species lilies, trumpets, and Orientals. The later-blooming Orientals have the biggest flowers and are apt to be top-heavy, but are the deliciously fragrant ones, so you might still want to try. Any pot-grown lily might benefit from a discrete staking job.

Unless you live in a mild climate, your potted lily bulbs may freeze to death over the winter. Consider them annuals, or transfer the bulbs into the ground and mulch come fall, and start over with new lily bulbs for your pots next spring.

GOOD CHOICES: Get bulbs of shorter-stemmed varieties. Asiatic 'Vermeer'; Orientals 'Con Amore' and 'Jet Set'.

Tulip
Tulipa species and hybrids
MATURE HEIGHT × WIDTH: 12-24 inches × 8-12 inches
FLOWER COLORS: many
FLOWER SIZE: 4-6 inches
BLOOM TIME: spring
SOIL: fertile, well drained
ZONES: 4-8, depending on variety

The queens of springtime are easy to grow in pots. Those of medium or shorter heights are obviously going to be easier to manage. If the stems and the flower display start to lean toward the sun, just turn the pot a quarter-turn each day to keep growth balanced and straight.

Get started in the fall, just as you do for in-ground tulip plantings. For best results, choose a sturdy pot with a drainage hole. Fill it with a decent, fertile growing mix. Plant a tulip bulb tip-up and shallowly. If you're planting several in one pot, it's okay to crowd them. Then keep the pot in a cool—not freezing—location for the winter months (covered with mulch or snugged into a cold frame).

As with daffodils, one potted springtime tulip show is typically all you can expect. After the first season, you could put the bulbs in the ground, but they may not return.

GOOD CHOICES: Consider some offbeat choices, such as the Greigiis, the viridifloras, and parrot tulips.

Other bulbs, corms, and tubers to try in containers:

- **Calla Lilies,** *Zantedeschia* cultivars
- **Cyclamen,** *Cyclamen persicum* as well as hardy species like *C. hederifolium* (top left)
- **Easter Lily,** *Lilium longiflorum*

- **Ornamental Onions,** *Allium giganteum* and myriad smaller-flowered ones (top right)
- **Pineapple Lily,** *Eucomis* species
- **Rain Lilies,** *Zephyranthes* species (center)

Cacti and Succulents

for everyone except those in the arid West and Southwest, growing cacti and succulents is mostly a container-gardening project. And even if you are in the right climate, it's a delight to have some potted ones around to admire at close range. The ones that are suitable are, of course, small compared to the giants of the desert and arroyos, and their charms are truly best appreciated where you can peer at them daily. Array some on a patio or deck; on a table; up ascending steps; or here and there out in the garden, if you can find suitable companions that do not overwhelm them.

The geometric or funky beauty of the plant itself is reason enough to raise a small cactus or succulent, but it's a real treat to witness one exploding into bloom with brilliant flowers, which can be an annual event. It was the late, great nature writer Edward Abbey who remarked that perhaps "life nowhere appears so full of color and promise as in the desert." Bringing that show up close and personal, in your own garden, is a true privilege and, well, exciting!

Ball Cactus, Sun Cup
Notocactus species
MATURE HEIGHT × **WIDTH: 3-5 inches** × **3-5 inches**
FLOWER COLORS: rose/white, red-orange, yellow
FLOWER SIZE: $1/2$-3 inches
BLOOM TIME: spring to early summer
SOIL: well-drained sandy loam

If you are new to cactus gardening, here's a good place to start. Available in small round shapes, these cute little cacti can easily be grown indoors or outside in a hot, bright spot. After five or more years, they gain a more columnar look.

The stems are generally light green and ridged, and often cloaked in a flurry of soft, interlocking spines. The flowers appear by summer, just one to a plant, at or near the top of the plant.

Watering is always a question with cacti, especially when you are hoping for flowers. Your best bet with this species is to let the soil become dry to the touch between waterings during the spring and summer. In the fall and winter, be more conservative, moistening only when the plant appears to shrivel. Keep it from freezing temperatures, and it can get by on as few as four hours of direct sunlight per day.

GOOD CHOICES: A cactus specialist will offer several but formally named cultivars don't seem to be marketed.

Barrel Cactus, Golden
Echinocactus grusonii
MATURE HEIGHT × **WIDTH: 6-15 inches** × **6-15 inches**
FLOWER COLORS: yellow
FLOWER SIZE: $2^1/2$ inches
BLOOM TIME: summer
SOIL: well-drained, sandy potting mix

This is another good cactus for beginners. It is very slow growing and very long-lived. The shape is plump and round, which looks good in a regular clay pot. It doesn't tend to bloom until it's reached a larger size, but that's okay (if it does, blooms are yellow and clustered at the crown, or top). A thick coating of golden spines against the plain green, ribbed barrel give the plant a glowing golden aura, especially when backlit by late-day sunlight—reason enough to delight in this attractive cactus.

Speaking of sunlight, it does fine with about four to six hours a day, maybe less than you'd expect for a cactus. Bring it indoors for the winter in cold climates and let it remain dormant in a cool room with several hours a day of indirect light. Water perhaps twice a month in warm weather, and cut back in winter.

GOOD CHOICES: Large barrel cactus, *Echinocactus ingens*.

CACTI AND SUCCULENTS

Burro Tail
Sedum morganianum
MATURE HEIGHT × WIDTH: 2- to 3-foot trailing stems
FLOWER COLORS: pink to deep red
FLOWER SIZE: 1/2 inch
BLOOM TIME: rare (in warm weather, if at all)
SOIL: well-drained, sandy potting mix

A cute name for a cute plant, burro tail is an easy-to-grow succulent. A trailing-stemmed member of the immense sedum family, it has numerous tiny leaves of grayish-green. The plant is a good choice for anywhere where you can let the ropelike "tails" hang down.

Its tightly packed leaves get even more crowded near the crown. Because they are the plant's oldest leaves, they shed first as the plant ages, leaving stems in the middle looking awkwardly bare. You can raise the plant higher so the trailing stems capture most of the attention, or you can begin again by cutting back the long stems and waiting for them to sprout again. And you could try rooting short sections of the part you cut off in the hopes of returning them to the main pot some day. (They will root in moist sand.)

Care is easy: plentiful sun, dry air, and only occasional watering, when the mix is quite dry to the touch.

GOOD CHOICES: 'Burrito' has fatter tails.

Hens and Chicks
Echeveria elegans
MATURE HEIGHT × WIDTH: up to 6 inches × 6 inches
FLOWER COLORS: pink and yellow
FLOWER SIZE: small, atop 6- to 8-inch stalks
BLOOM TIME: summer
SOIL: well-drained, sandy potting soil

You can't just have one plant, as the common name hints! First there's a rosette of thick little succulent gray-green leaves and before you know it, baby plants are popping up right beside it. That's why a pot always ends up becoming a potful.

Since they originally hail from the deserts of Mexico, hens and chicks are tough and thrive in a potting mix liberally enriched with sand; they don't need much water, and they love sunshine.

To move the baby plants into their own pot, just cut them away with a sharp, clean knife and extract their roots with care. Make sure their new home is initially moist, though with the same mixture of light potting mix and sand that they had before. Really tiny ones can be placed in really small pots—this is a fun project for a child.

GOOD CHOICES: Other, similar rosette-forming succulents go by the same common name, including *Echeveria imbricata* and *E. secunda*.

Jade Plant
Crassula argentea
MATURE HEIGHT × WIDTH: varies
FLOWER COLORS: white or pink
FLOWER SIZE: star-shaped, small clusters
BLOOM TIME: winter
SOIL: well-drained, sandy potting soil

To really appreciate jade plant's unique features and unique beauty, your best bet is to enjoy it in a pot. This way, it also stays a manageable size.

It gets its common name from the color of the unusual leaves, which, when the plant is healthy and well grown, are quite a lovely, subtle shade of jade green. The more sun this plant gets, the better—and when it is getting good doses, the leaves respond by having red rims around the edges. Plentiful sun also prompts jade plant to flower, in a flurry of little white clusters atop slender stems.

A jade plant gets stressed and looks poorly not when you neglect it, but when you lavish too much care on it. Specifically, the only time you should water is when the fat, moisture-conserving leaves are visibly shriveled.

GOOD CHOICES: Jade plant cultivars include 'Sunset' with yellowish leaves tinged with red; 'Crosby's Dwarf', a nearly cascading low, compact grower; and the stunning 'Tricolor' with green, white, and pinkish variegation.

Kalanchoe
Kalanchoe blossfeldiana
MATURE HEIGHT × WIDTH: 6-14 inches × 6-14 inches
FLOWER COLORS: red, orange, pink, mauve, yellow
FLOWER SIZE: 2- to 4-inch wide clusters
BLOOM TIME: spring
SOIL: well-drained potting soil

Cheery, bright flowers in sprays atop stalks are the main attraction of this agreeable succulent. Though they come in a variety of colors, a fiery orange-red is the one you see most. This plant can really brighten up a room or outdoor display in the company of non-flowering succulents and cacti. They have the added virtue of being fairly long lasting.

In order to bloom, kalanchoe needs the same conditions it gets in its native desert habitat: shorter days and cooler temperatures. The flowers then burst forth. Water weekly, when the plant is in bud and flower, and more often in hot weather (give your plant a drink whenever the top of the soil mix gets dry). Bright but indirect light, indoors or out, is ideal. If you put your kalanchoe outdoors, be on the lookout for slugs and snails, which like to nibble the leaves. That said, this is basically a very easy, easygoing plant.

GOOD CHOICES: There are literally dozens of different cultivars; just choose the color you like.

Live-forever, Pinwheel

Aeonium haworthii

MATURE HEIGHT × **WIDTH: up to 1-2 feet × 1-2 feet**
FLOWER COLORS: white or pale yellow, tinged pink
FLOWER SIZE: 4- to 5-inch long clusters
BLOOM TIME: early spring
SOIL: well-drained, sandy potting soil

The big draw is its colorful leaves, which are more than the typical, plain gray-green. Every leaf is rimmed in maroon-red; if you look closely, it's actually a tiny ruff of bristles that bear the contrasting color. Viewed from further away, this feature gives the rosettes stylish definition. Also, the leaves develop an intriguing powdery, waxy coating in the summer months.

Flowers, if they appear, come in early spring, after a slowed-down winter period of reduced water and lower temperatures. They arise in jaunty clusters atop slender stems and are usually white or pale yellow, tinged with pink. A grouping of these plants in bloom is quite a pretty sight.

Unlike some succulents, this one is a fast grower. It thrives in full sun and low humidity and little water. Divide and repot in late winter or early spring, just before new growth begins for the year. Water lightly until new roots and leaves develop.

GOOD CHOICES: The closely related "black tree," *Aeonium arboreum* 'Atropurpureum'.

Pincushion Cactus

Mammillaria species and cultivars

MATURE HEIGHT × **WIDTH: up to 8 inches × 8 inches**
FLOWER COLORS: cream, yellow, pink, red
FLOWER SIZE: $3/4$ inch
BLOOM TIME: spring or summer
SOIL: well-drained potting soil

If you want a cactus that produces flowers, this is an excellent choice. There are more than 350 species, primarily in the cream, yellow, and pink-red range. These flowers appear every spring or summer, depending on the weather. They form a ring around the top of the plant, like a baby girl's bonnet.

This cactus typically has a roundish profile. There are no ribs, but rather protuberances on the stems, with spines at the very tips. Though they cloak the plant, the spines are never unfriendly—some species sport a mass of white fibers, others have hooked spines, and some are so closely knit that they are known as "huggables" because they can't poke you.

Care for all species is essentially the same, and quite easy. Pincushion cacti like about three hours of direct sun per day. You can water weekly or biweekly, more during the warm months and less during the cool ones.

GOOD CHOICES: *Mammillaria candida*, the snowball pincushion; *M. parkinsonii*, called owl eyes.

Other cacti and succulents to try in containers:

- **Agave,** *Agave* species and cultivars (top left)
- **Fairy Washboard,** *Haworthia fasciata*
- **Christmas Cactus,** *Schlumbergera bridgesii* and hybrids
- **Living Stones,** *Lithops* species (center)
- **Mexican Old-Man Cactus,** *Cephalocereus senilis*

- **Night-blooming Cereus,** *Hylocereus undatus* (top right)
- **Orchid Cactus,** *Epiphyllum* hybrids
- **Peanut Cactus,** *Chamaecereus silvestri*
- **Rattail Cactus,** *Aporocactus flagelliformis*
- **String-of-Beads,** *Senecio rowleyanus*

Herbs

few plants are as easy or as satisfactory in containers as herbs. This is because most are fairly simple to grow, asking little more than a nice, sunny spot. That spot can be on your kitchen windowsill—so cooking herbs are conveniently close at hand and always wonderfully fresh. Or it can be on a balcony, deck, patio, or porch, anywhere that is somewhat sheltered from drying winds, very hot sun, and foot traffic.

Pot-grown herbs, whether grown individually or in a small group, tend not to be very large plants. For this reason, it is nice to cluster them, or raise them up so they still get noticed (on a table, shelf, or pedestal). While not as flashy as, say, flowering annuals or tropical plants, herbs are attractive in their own right. There is great variety in leaf form and even leaf color, plus you often get the bonus of appealing fragrance. Herb flowers may not appear or may not be conspicuous, so bring color to your herb collection by growing the plants in pretty pots or combining them with flowering plants, or both.

Snipping branches off your pot-grown herbs, either for use in recipes or for some decorative purpose (a mixed bouquet, say, or even a sprig tucked under the ribbon of a wrapped gift), is a smart practice. It slows down the going-to-seed process; some herbs get lanky or lose their pungency once they "bolt" or produce seed. Trimming your herb plants has another practical purpose—it keeps them tidy and compact, so they continue to look handsome throughout the growing season.

Aloe
Aloe vera (A. *barbadensis*)
MATURE HEIGHT × WIDTH: 1-2 feet × 1-2 feet
FLOWER COLORS: n/a
FLOWER SIZE: n/a
BLOOM TIME: n/a
SOIL: well drained, even dry
ZONE: 10

Here is a plant that asks very little and gives a lot. A single specimen in a pot on a windowsill will thrive despite minimal water, gritty soil, and less than a full day of sun. In fact, aloe seems to prosper on neglect, growing quite slowly but sometimes developing little "pup" plants around its base. (These are easily separated and repotted to give away to friends!) The succulent leaves are a cool or olive-green, barely toothed, and never marred by pests or diseases. When you snap one off, both sides immediately bleed a sticky sap that brings fast relief to minor kitchen burns, as well as to itchy skin, sunburns, cuts, and abrasions.

An ancient plant, said to be native to Africa, aloe is deservedly popular far and wide to this very day. Even "black thumb" gardeners have no trouble growing one. It's an attractive and undeniably useful plant to have around.

GOOD CHOICES: There are no cultivars, though you may notice some variation in leaf color.

Basil
Ocimum basilicum
MATURE HEIGHT × WIDTH: 2 feet × 1 foot
FLOWER COLORS: white, lavender
FLOWER SIZE: small 1- to 2-inch spires
BLOOM TIME: summer
SOIL: rich, moist, well drained
ZONE: 10

Freshly picked basil is one of summer's great pleasures, whether you are making pesto or tossing some into a pasta dish or salad. It is not difficult to grow. Harvest often, because cutting back help keeps the fast-growing plant in bounds. If flowers appear, pinch them off so the plant's energy is not diverted to them.

The classic, favorite basil has large, broad, somewhat crinkly leaves. If you go hunting in seed catalogs or visit a specialty herb nursery, you'll be captivated by the wide range of other basils. It would be fun to grow several different kinds and try them in various recipes.

For best flavor, site your basil in full sun and don't let it dry out. Freshly harvested leaves are superior to dried. If you have surplus snipped-off leaves, roll them (clean and dry) in paper towels and freeze them in plastic bags.

GOOD CHOICES: 'Dwarf Bush' and 'Genovese Compact' for small pots. For larger containers: 1998 All-America Selections winner 'Sweet Dani Lemon' and 2002 AAS winner 'Magical Michael'.

Chives
Allium schoenoprasum
MATURE HEIGHT × WIDTH: 1-1¹/₂ feet × up to 1 foot
FLOWER COLORS: pink to lavender
FLOWER SIZE: ¹/₂ inch
BLOOM TIME: early summer
SOIL: average to rich, well drained
ZONES: 3-9

This is one of the most attractive herbs, abounding in small-ish, perky, globe-shaped flowers starting in early summer. They're accompanied by tufts of grassy, hollow leaves that, owing to their sturdy nature and short height, don't tend to flop over. So chives make a very handsome pot plant.

The plant is perfectly edible, and its mild-flavored snippings make a welcome addition to salads, soups, and spreads. What you may not know is that the flowers are also edible and can contribute to the same dishes. Dried-flower arrangers like the flowers because they keep their shape and color fairly well and don't shatter.

Unlike some other members of the onion and garlic family, chives doesn't have a long natural dormant period. If you garden in a mild climate, you can harvest year-round. In cold-winter areas, bring the pots inside and keep them on a sunny windowsill. When you're serving baked potatoes with dinner on some frosty night, you'll be glad you did.

GOOD CHOICES: 'Forescate'; for heftier stems, 'Staro'.

Dill
Anthemum graveolens
MATURE HEIGHT × WIDTH: 1-3 feet × 1-2 feet
FLOWER COLORS: yellow
FLOWER SIZE: 4-6 inches
BLOOM TIME: summer
SOIL: average, well drained
ZONES: all (annual)

In the yard, dill can be a tall and sprawling plant. But it is certainly possible to grow it in a pot, and the dwarf varieties are particularly successful. Dill likes plenty of sun, so set the container in a bright, warm spot.

The key to success is not to overwater, which leads to floppy growth and root rot. Water only when the soil surface begins to dry.

You can keep the plant both productive and attractive by removing entire stems as needed. Your best bet is cut them right when you need them; the flavor will be the most delicious and intense. Sprinkle the leaves into leafy salads or potato salad, add to fish dishes, or include in steamed or stir-fried vegetable recipes. Dill is especially tasty with tomatoes. A wonderful combination in a container—as well as in a meal—is a dill plant paired with one of the bush cherry tomato varieties.

GOOD CHOICES: An excellent dwarf variety is 1992 All-America Selections winner 'Fern Leaf'; intensely flavored 'Dukat'; old favorite 'Bouquet'.

Feverfew
Tanacetum parthenium
MATURE HEIGHT × WIDTH: 1-3 feet × 1-3 feet
FLOWER COLORS: white
FLOWER SIZE: 1/2 inch
BLOOM TIME: summer
SOIL: average, well drained
ZONES: 5-9

With its perky little daisies and compact, bushy growth habit, feverfew is an excellent candidate for a pot or window box. The flowers are also fairly durable, standing up to summer heat and then weathering fall's cooler, damper weather. All it really asks is well-drained soil to grow in; it performs well in full sun and partial shade.

Feverfew flowers are also plentiful. Below the flowers are the medium-green, aromatic leaves, reminiscent of mum foliage (a relative). Pinch flowers and leaves periodically to keep the plant well-shaped and in bounds.

This herb gets its name from its long-standing reputation as a fever reducer, though modern science has not confirmed its efficacy. However, it turns out that the leaves have anti-inflammatory properties, which is why you see feverfew tablets in the local health-food store or pharmacy. Don't try ingesting the leaves of your homegrown plant; it's not safe and besides, their flavor is strong and bitter.

GOOD CHOICES: Try a double-flowered 'Ball's Double White' or 'Snowball'; 'Santana' is an excellent dwarf.

Geranium, Scented
Pelargonium species and hybrids
MATURE HEIGHT × WIDTH: 1-2 feet × 1-2 feet
FLOWER COLORS: pink, white
FLOWER SIZE: varies
BLOOM TIME: summer
SOIL: well drained
ZONES: 9-10

These are not the showy-flowered geraniums of window boxes, but rather a separate group of related plants treasured for their uniquely scented leaves. The leaves may look much the same as regular geraniums, but the texture is often softer, even felted to the touch. Leaf color varies, from dark emerald green to lime green with splashes or touches of other colors.

These geraniums radiate wonderful fragrance. Grown in a clay pot or something more decorative, they never fail to charm. They're nice solo, or combine well with a smaller, trailing flowering plants.

When you pinch off leaves, you can dry them for use in homemade potpourri or sachets. Fresh-picked rose-scented geranium leaves are a classic addition to apple jelly. Some cooks like to toss a few leaves into their sugar canister to enhance their baked treats.

GOOD CHOICES: Apple (*P. odoratissimum*), chocolate peppermint (a hybrid), lemon (*P. crispum*), and rose (*P. graveolens*).

Lavender
Lavandula species and cultivars
MATURE HEIGHT × WIDTH: 1-3 feet × 1-3 feet
FLOWER COLORS: lavender
FLOWER SIZE: 6- to 8-inch spires
BLOOM TIME: early to midsummer
SOIL: light, well-drained, slightly alkaline
ZONES: 5-8

So enchanting is its fragrance and so easy is it to grow, that lavender has become deservedly popular. Nurseries have responded by seeking out and stocking a wider range of choices, and some of the newer or offbeat lavender offerings are excellent in pots. They're smaller, more compact, have prettier flowers . . . and, of course, sport that haunting scent. So peruse a range of choices before selecting the one (or ones) you will grow.

In order to thrive, however, lavender needs the right soil mix. A lighter medium, billed as slightly alkaline or to which you have mixed in some lime dust, is best. Don't overwater, or the roots may rot.

Once your lavender begins to flower, start picking. It's the moment you've been waiting for, plus trimming induces the plant to keep on blooming. Tuck the stems into flower arrangements, or dry them for use in potpourri or cooking.

GOOD CHOICES: *L. angustifolia* 'Lavenite Petite'; 'Nana Atropurpurea'.

Marjoram
Origanum majorana
MATURE HEIGHT × WIDTH: 1-2 feet × 1-2 feet
FLOWER COLORS: white or pink
FLOWER SIZE: tiny
BLOOM TIME: midsummer
SOIL: well drained, slightly alkaline
ZONES: 6-9

Although sometimes mistaken for oregano, marjoram is different from that close relative. Marjoram leaves are sweeter and more balsamlike. Anyone who likes to cook should keep a pot around. Sprinkle the leaves into homemade chicken soup, Italian dishes where you might normally use oregano, and omelets and frittatas. It's also terrific in lamb dishes. When you cut it back, not to worry— new growth appears quickly.

Another reason to grow this herb in a pot is the fact that it is somewhat tender; cold or freezing weather invariably kills it. Marjoram is a slow grower, so it tends to stay a manageable size for you in its container.

For best flavor, put your pot of marjoram in a hot, sunny spot, and water sparingly but regularly so the soil mix is never soggy. Leaves harvested just as the flowers appear have the best flavor. And marjoram leaves keep their splendid, unique flavor even when dried.

GOOD CHOICES: *O. × majoricum* is a more cold-hardy hybrid with especially sweet-scented leaves.

Mint
Mentha species and cultivars
MATURE HEIGHT × WIDTH: 1-3 feet × 1-3 feet
FLOWER COLORS: white, pink, lavender
FLOWER SIZE: tiny spikes
BLOOM TIME: midsummer
SOIL: moist, fertile
ZONES: 5-9

If ever there was an herb that should be grown in a container, it is mint. This is because mint is such a rampant grower, particularly when it gets the moist, fertile soil it loves.

And it is a pretty and tasty herb. The leaves are rarely marred by any pest or disease, and they retain a crisp texture and handsome color for months on end. Their flavor is refreshing, in everything from summer salads and tabouli to drinks like mint juleps and iced tea. No doubt about it, it's great to have mint around, and a potful will certainly provide you with all the leaves you want and need.

For flavor variations, check a good nursery or seed catalog—you'll be astounded by the many choices. But no matter what kind of mint you grow, you'll be glad to keep it confined to a pot.

GOOD CHOICES: Huge range of choices—there is sometimes name and proper identification confusion, so just go ahead and choose what appeals to you.

Oregano
Origanum vulgare
MATURE HEIGHT × WIDTH: 1-3 feet × 1-3 feet
FLOWER COLORS: pink
FLOWER SIZE: tiny
BLOOM TIME: midsummer
SOIL: decent, well drained
ZONES: 5-9

Growing your own oregano guarantees the best flavor. Sun-warmed and just-picked leaves are a total pleasure when you crush them between your fingers: The delicious, pungent, almost peppery scent just radiates. And there's no match for freshly snipped oregano in any favorite recipe. Dried oregano just can't begin to equal the rich taste of fresh.

For best results, place your pot of oregano in a hot, sunny spot that mimics its native growing conditions on the bright, dry hillsides of the Mediterranean. This increases the oil content in the leaves for a superb harvest.

Another plus is that oregano is attractive. The plant is naturally variable in terms of leaf size and color, which gives its robust growth a touch of exuberance. Horticulturists have also selected out attractive-leaved variations (yellow leaves, for instance, as well as white-rimmed ones) that are good-looking in their own right and also blend well with other herbs or even flowers in a mixed pot or window box display.

GOOD CHOICES: "Greek" oregano, a strain reputed to have stronger, richer flavor than the species.

Parsley
Petroselinum crispum
MATURE HEIGHT × WIDTH: 1-3 feet × 1-3 feet
FLOWER COLORS: greenish-yellow
FLOWER SIZE: tiny umbels
BLOOM TIME: summer
SOIL: average, well drained
ZONES: 4-9

Homegrown parsley prospers in a pot. It looks attractive all season long and well into fall, for it is cold hardy. Grow it solo, or try its bright green foliage as a companion to flowers such as miniature roses or nasturtiums.

Whatever you decide, site it in a sunny spot, and remember to water regularly. Your parsley will respond with abundant foliage. Harvest outer leaves and the center of the plant will soon generate new growth. (The flowers should be snipped off when they appear, so the plant continues to concentrate its energy on leaves.)

There are two main kinds of parsley. The species is known as "curly leaf"; closely related "flat leaf" is *P. crispum* var. *neopolitanum*. Experienced cooks will tell you that the latter has a more robust, richer flavor. As a result, it dries better, though fresh parsley is always preferable. Too often dismissed as a mere garnish, parsley is vitamin-packed (vitamins A and C, plus some B vitamins, iron, and calcium).

GOOD CHOICES: Flat leaf parsley (*P. crispum* var. *neopolitanum*); 'Italian Dark Green'.

Rosemary
Rosmarinus officinalis
MATURE HEIGHT × WIDTH: 1-6 feet × 1-6 feet
FLOWER COLORS: blue or pink
FLOWER SIZE: tiny
BLOOM TIME: summer
SOIL: light to average, well drained
ZONES: 8-10

The piney scent of rosemary is seductive on a warm summer day, and even more so when the pot is sited where you pass by or spend time. It is also one of the prettiest herbs to grow in a container, and will remain bushy if you pinch and prune often—a pleasant chore! The most fragrant and flavorful leaves are produced before the plant begins to flower.

Rosemary is vulnerable to root rot, so grow it in a light, even sandy medium that drains well. If the needlelike leaves develop brown tips, you are overwatering or the mix is too heavy and is retaining too much moisture. Repot every spring, or whenever you notice the plant showing signs of crowding (yellowed leaves and woody growth).

This beautiful herb hails from the Mediterranean and should be given plenty of sun. If you grow rosemary in a clay or terra-cotta pot, it looks perfectly at home.

GOOD CHOICES: A compact, new introduction is *R. officinalis* ssp. *prostratus* 'Baby PJ'; 'Irene' is an outstanding trailing form.

Sage
Salvia officinalis
MATURE HEIGHT × WIDTH: 1-2¹/₂ feet × 1-2 feet
FLOWER COLORS: pink, purple, or white
FLOWER SIZE: tiny
BLOOM TIME: summer
SOIL: average, well drained
ZONES: 4-8

Here's an herb you can rely on to do double duty. The plant is very handsome, and some of its cultivars even more so, with variegated and rimmed leaves. It is also very productive, generating plenty of aromatic, tasty leaves that are never marred by pests or diseases. Indeed, sage is easy to grow and can even withstand some neglect. It usually remains productive for two seasons. Its second spring, you'd be wise to prune it back hard so you can get some new growth.

Flower spikes appear in midsummer and the color varies, depending on which one you are growing. If you leave them on the plant, bees, butterflies, and even hummingbirds may flit by for a visit.

Fresh sage leaves are wonderful to have for all sorts of dishes, from vegetables and casseroles to egg dishes and soups. The leaves dry well, but the flavor changes, becoming less subtle. The flowers are perfectly edible as well.

GOOD CHOICES: Multicolor-leaved 'Tricolor'; yellow-variegated-leaf dwarf variety 'Aurea'; 'Berggarten' with rounded silvery leaves.

Summer Savory
Satureja hortensis
MATURE HEIGHT × WIDTH: 1-1¹/₂ feet × 1-1¹/₂ feet
FLOWER COLORS: white, pale pink
FLOWER SIZE: tiny
BLOOM TIME: summer
SOIL: average, well drained
ZONES: all (annual)

You won't often find this herb at the market, but once you grow it at home, you'll wonder why it isn't everywhere. The versatile flavor is a bit like thyme, but more peppery. It goes great especially in vegetable dishes, and also herb butters and potato salad.

Summer savory grows well in a pot, making a nice little bush covered in soft, petite leaves of gray-green. They zip off a stem easily and need not be minced when added to recipes. The tiny flowers appear around the middle of the summer in small clusters in the upper leaf axils. Depending on the location of your container, browsing bees may take notice.

This is one herb that is quick and easy from seed, and you can certainly find a packet from whatever seed catalog you usually order your vegetable seeds. It's an annual, so you'll have to start over each year, but once you're hooked, summer savory will stay on your list.

GOOD CHOICES: Short, sturdy 'Aromata' has more intense aroma and peppery taste.

Tarragon
Artemisia dracunculus
MATURE HEIGHT × WIDTH: 1-2 feet × 1-2 feet
FLOWER COLORS: pale yellow, greenish-white
FLOWER SIZE: tiny panicles
BLOOM TIME: summer
SOIL: average, well drained
ZONES: 4-9

Though not as attractive or compact as some other herbs, tarragon is so valuable in the kitchen that you ought to grow it anyway. If appearance is important, just grow it in a distinctive or colorful pot, or add it to a container or window box that includes sun-loving flowers. (Its own flowers, if they appear, should be clipped off so leaf production continues.) Whatever you decide, make sure there is good drainage, for root rot can be fatal for tarragon.

This is an assertive herb whose flavor is tangy and sharp. It's part of the delicious herb mixture known as *fines herbes* (along with parsley and chervil) and is indispensable in sauces such as béarnaise, hollandaise, and tartar. Tarragon is also excellent added to mayonnaise, herb butter, and salad dressings. It's a popular ingredient in fish, chicken, and veal dishes as well.

Tarragon leaves are much tastier fresh than dried. Pick them right before you need them or at least on the same day.

GOOD CHOICES: "Russian tarragon" is more vigorous and cold hardy.

Thyme
Thymus species and cultivars
MATURE HEIGHT × WIDTH: 6-12 inches × 6-12 inches
FLOWER COLORS: lavender, pink
FLOWER SIZE: tiny, tubular-shaped
BLOOM TIME: summer
SOIL: average, well drained
ZONES: 5-9

A dense, tiny-leaved, low-growing plant, thyme is often used in the garden as a groundcover or inserted between paving stones on a terrace. But its compact growth habit also makes it suitable for growing in containers, either on its own or at the feet of more erect herbs or flowers. It must have well-drained mix, however, or the roots will rot.

Thyme is so prolific that you can harvest snippings often. The species is quite easy to grow and justifiably popular, and herb specialists may tempt you with some interesting variations, including lemon thyme and caraway thyme. Creeping thyme will spill out over the rim of a bigger pot or urn. All variations, like the species, do best if the pot is placed in a warm, sunny location.

Fresh-picked thyme is terrific in meat, game, and poultry dishes. It retains good flavor when dried, so you can add it to soups and casseroles during the winter months.

GOOD CHOICES: Lemon thyme (*T. citriodorus*), caraway thyme (*T. herba-barona*), creeping thyme (*T. praecox* ssp. *arcticus*).

Other herbs to try in containers:

- **Chervil,** *Anthriscus cerefolium* (top left)
- **Garlic Chives,** *Allium tuberosum* (top right)
- **Lemon Balm,** *Melissa officinalis* (center)
- **Lemongrass,** *Cymbopogon citratus*

- **Mint Marigold,** *Tagetes lucida*
- **Pepper, Ornamental,** *Capsicum annuum*
- **Pot Marigold,** *Calendula officinalis*
- **Winter Savory,** *Satureja montana*

Indoor Plants or Houseplants

raising potted plants indoors can be an introduction to gardening, a shot at having a green thumb, or simply a way to connect with growing things. This is especially true for apartment-dwellers, but applies to anyone who is either very busy, doesn't have much of a yard to garden in, or just wants to enjoy indoor horticulture. Whatever the reason, the pleasure is undeniable—it's an opportunity to enjoy nature up close.

Houseplants need not be difficult or tricky. They're all native to some place and the key is to have or to provide growing conditions similar to the place where they grow wild. If you choose wisely and provide adequate care, a plant should thrive in your home's light, temperature, and humidity conditions. Also, most are tougher than you think.

Nor do "easy" or "can't miss" ones have to be dull or plain-looking plants; peruse the entries that follow and you may be pleasantly surprised to find appealing options you hadn't considered. Some produce beautiful or intriguing flowers and even contribute fragrance to your home, delighting you and other observers with a fascinating annual cycle. In any event, there are wonderful worlds to explore with indoor plants, and your journey begins here.

African Violet
Saintpaulia hybrids
MATURE HEIGHT × WIDTH:
FLOWER COLORS: purple and pink, red, white
FLOWER SIZE: 1-2 inches
BLOOM TIME: year-round
SOIL: well-drained potting soil

African violets are so familiar that gardeners may dismiss them, and thereby miss out on the improvements and innovations of recent years. And these sturdy houseplants also suffer from a misconception that they are tricky to grow.

Actually, they mostly need the right light conditions. A south or west window is ideal because blazing direct light can be harmful. If conditions are less than perfect, choose a tougher type—the ones with plain (not ruffled) leaves or the ones that are green on top and silvery below (as opposed to green on top and red below).

Water when the top of the soil mix is dry. Avoid letting the leaves get wet, as spots will appear. You can raise humidity either by placing the pot on a saucer of pebbles or grouping several plants together. For plentiful flowers, feed your plant regularly with a standard houseplant food.

GOOD CHOICES: You're at the mercy of whatever local nurseries stock; or hook up with members of the nearest chapter of the African Violet Society of America.

Aluminum Plant
Pilea cadierei
MATURE HEIGHT × WIDTH: 1-1$\frac{1}{2}$ feet × 1-1$\frac{1}{2}$ feet
FLOWER COLORS: n/a
FLOWER SIZE: tiny, rare
BLOOM TIME: n/a
SOIL: well-drained potting soil

The odd common name comes from the impression somebody, somewhere got that the oval-shaped, silver-blotched leaves look as though they've been dunked in aluminum paint. That seems a bit of a stretch, and you have to wonder what folks call this plant back in its native tropics. Nonetheless, the silvery coloration is its main attraction and is best appreciated in bright, filtered light. A fancy pot is a fine idea, too.

This plant also has a tendency to get lanky and leggy over time, so keep it pinched back for as long as this is practical. (After a few years, you may decide to start over by taking cuttings of the original plant; stem cuttings root readily.)

Another way to keep this handsome plant looking its best is to offer extra humidity, either with trays containing pebbles for its pot to rest on, regular spritzing, or even a spot in a terrarium. Water it more in hot weather, and less in cool.

GOOD CHOICES: No cultivars, but the related *Pilea involucrata* has seersucker-textured, smaller leaves.

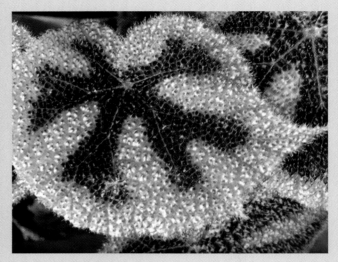

Aralia, Japanese
Fatsia japonica
MATURE HEIGHT × WIDTH: 5-8 feet × 3-6 feet
FLOWER COLORS: white
FLOWER SIZE: small roundish clusters
BLOOM TIME: fall
SOIL: well-drained potting soil

This bold-looking, easygoing plant is happiest when it is an indoor-outdoor plant. In other words, drag its pot outside for the warm months, and haul it back in when cold weather returns. Indoors or out, it cheerfully displays rich green, glossy-textured leaves arising from a central stem. They look a lot like fig leaves (the edible kind of fig, that is), which accounts for its other common name, "figleaf palm," though it is not a palm either.

Unlike some houseplants, aralia is fine with cooler temperatures (if it starts shedding leaves, the problem is probably too much warmth). Nor does it want bright sunshine. If you keep it inside, indirect light is good; outdoors, a spot in filtered shade is desirable. You may mist it occasionally for a little extra humidity, though this is not necessary if the plant seems to be thriving otherwise. Keep the soil slightly moist and a bit drier during the winter months.

GOOD CHOICES: 'Moseri' is a lower-growing, more compact version; the leaves of 'Variegata' are edged golden yellow to creamy white.

Begonia, Rex
Begonia × rex-cultorum
MATURE HEIGHT × WIDTH: 8-12 inches × 8-12 inches
FLOWER COLORS: white, pink
FLOWER SIZE: tiny, in sprays
BLOOM TIME: winter
SOIL: light, well-drained potting mix

While all begonias have nice foliage, those of the "rex" group are the most gorgeous. Every imaginable variation on maroon, black, ruby red, emerald green, and silver can be found in this group. Sometimes a slender spray of tiny white or pink flowers arises, but these are by no means the main attraction.

Because the leaves are so beautiful, you'd be wise to grow your rex begonia in a plain pot to avoid distracting from the show. Clay pots are a good choice because their warm reddish hue flatters any red, maroon, or purple leaf coloration.

Rex begonias do best in a warm room (more than 60 degrees) and thrive on at least 50 percent humidity. A light potting mix is fine, and don't overdo watering, because soggy soil leads to rot. Bright sunshine is not necessary; an east- or west-facing window is perfect. In return, your rex will turn out to be the most splendid begonia plant you've ever had the pleasure of growing.

GOOD CHOICES: 'Ember', 'Beau Rouge', and 'Fantasy'.

Cast Iron Plant
Aspidistra eliator
MATURE HEIGHT × WIDTH: 1-2¹/₂ feet × 1-2¹/₂ feet
FLOWER COLORS: brownish
FLOWER SIZE: inconspicuous
BLOOM TIME: spring
SOIL: well-drained potting soil

This stalwart withstands neglect better than almost any other houseplant save a cactus. You can place it almost anywhere, regardless of light—it's that adaptable. Nor does it care about temperature (although, obviously, don't stick it outside in freezing weather). Water only every now and then. Fertilizing is never necessary.

Cast iron plant is very slow growing, which is the key to its undemanding nature. This also means that you should purchase one that's about the size you want, for things won't change much. The only time you ever see new leaves is when they unfurl, slowly, of course, at just about the time a very old leaf is fading away.

The broad, flat leaves are a nice dark green that lends a lush look to wherever you decide to display the plant. Should you wish to get an especially luxurious perform-ance, try an occasional spritz of water to boost humidity and regular fertilizing during the warm months. The leaves tend to get dusty, so wipe them down occasionally.

GOOD CHOICES: 'Variegata' has white-striped leaves.

Chinese Evergreen
Aglaonema modestum (simplex)
MATURE HEIGHT × WIDTH: 2-3 feet × 1-2 feet
FLOWER COLORS: green-white
FLOWER SIZE: small spathes
BLOOM TIME: winter-spring (rare)
SOIL: well-drained, rich potting soil

This handsome favorite tolerates all kinds of light condi-tions, including the low light of a dim or windowless room.

Hailing from the humid jungles of Southeast Asia and China, Chinese evergreen does like to be warm and a bit humid. So don't let the temperatures drop below 60 degrees and spritz the leaves every now and then.

In return for this minimal care, the plant is always obligingly good-looking. Its one flaw is its tendency to, over time, grow tall and gangly as it loses its lower leaves. When this happens, you can cut it back partway and the stem will generate new growth. The chopped-off top can be easily rooted in a glass of water and then returned to the same pot or started in a new one.

One caveat: Sap may form and drip off the tips of the leaves, so don't display the pot on a wood surface or place it on a mat.

GOOD CHOICES: The foliage of 'Silver King' is strongly marked with silver.

Corn Plant
Dracaena species and cultivars
MATURE HEIGHT × WIDTH: varies with species
FLOWER COLORS: n/a
FLOWER SIZE: n/a
BLOOM TIME: n/a
SOIL: well-drained potting soil

Though dragon plants grow to impressive, tree-like sizes in their native Africa, Asia, and Pacific Islands, potted in your home or on your deck, what you get is a much shorter version. And yet they retain a treelike habit, always tending toward a long, bare stem with foliage at the top.

If you buy a larger plant, as opposed to a little table-top-size one, you'll probably get one that's been tinkered with already. Growers like to cut off the top when the plant is a few feet high and let new growth sprout. The result is some side growth that eventually also tries to head skyward. In the end, these plants get a sort of endearing "Dr. Seuss tree" look.

A spot in bright but indirect light, out of the wind, is best. Mild, average temperatures are fine. The soil mix ought to be slightly on the dry side (overwatering is a common mistake).

GOOD CHOICES: The "ribbon plant" (*Dracaena deremensis*); 'Warneckii'; "corn plant" (*Dracaena fragrans*); 'Massangeana'; "red-margined" dragon tree (*Dracaena marginata*) and its cultivar 'Tricolor'.

Peperomia
Peperomia species and cultivars
MATURE HEIGHT × WIDTH: up to 1 foot × 1 foot
FLOWER COLORS: white
FLOWER SIZE: slender, inconspicuous 4-inch spike
BLOOM TIME: winter to spring
SOIL: well-drained potting soil

This is a big group of slow-growing houseplants prized for their handsome leaves and agreeable personalities. Peperomia stems and leaves are somewhat succulent, which means that the plants can survive with only occasional watering. When in doubt, water less, not more. Nor are they fussy about humidity; you don't have to spritz them or keep their pots on a tray of pebbles as you do some houseplants.

Their main requirement is the right potting soil. They don't like to be soggy, and will rot and die when overwatered. So stir a handful of sand or perlite in regular potting soil. Peperomias also have rather shallow root systems, which means you can grow them in shallow, broad containers if you wish.

If you'd like to display peperomias with other plants, they get along well with others of their kind—or their pots can be arrayed at the feet of other houseplants or annuals in larger pots.

GOOD CHOICES: *Peperomia caperata* 'Emerald Ripple'; for color, *Peperomia obtusifolia*.

Philodendron
Philodendron species and cultivars
MATURE HEIGHT × WIDTH: varies
FLOWER COLORS: greenish, white, reddish bracts
FLOWER SIZE: small spathes
BLOOM TIME: rare, but winter or spring
SOIL: well-drained potting soil

"Philo" is "love" and "dendron" means tree, which adds up to "tree-loving" for this popular plant. The species is native to the thick, overgrown jungles of Central America, and in that setting philodendrons tend to be vines that ramble along the forest floor and mount trees. A vining one in your home will grab on to a support, so insert a sturdy wooden stick right in the pot, and then cut back the stem when it reaches the top for some lateral growth. Alternatively, in a hanging basket, they will trail down.

The stems of bushy philodendrons, on the other hand, emerge from a central crown or trunk and display one leaf per. Over time, individual leaves get quite large, until you have a fairly substantial plant.

All philodendrons may be set outdoors in mild weather, preferring indirect sun and tolerating partial or even full shade. Water sparingly.

GOOD CHOICES: The best vining type is heartleaf, *Philodendron oxycardium* (or *P. cordatum*). A classic bushy one is "saddleleaf," *Philodendron selloum*. And there are many more!

Ponytail Palm
Beaucarnea recurvata
MATURE HEIGHT × WIDTH: 3-4 feet × 3-4 feet
FLOWER COLORS: creamy white
FLOWER SIZE: small clusters
BLOOM TIME: rare
SOIL: well-drained potting soil

Without a doubt, this is one of the more exotic-looking houseplants! The first thing you notice is the brown, bulbous base, which rests partly above the soil surface, and actually is not stem tissue but root. From the top of this emerges the gracefully arching, grass-thin leaves. They can eventually hang down to a length of 3 or 4 feet. Before this happens, you will want to display this plant in such a way that this fountain of foliage is shown off well. Give it a substantial pot so it doesn't topple over, and don't crowd other pots around it. Some gardeners like to elevate their pot of ponytail palm on a pedestal, which works.

Care is easy. The huge root stores water, helping the plant through dry spells or your neglect. You can get away with watering it only once a month. It tolerates low light and doesn't have special humidity requirements, though it does like to be warm. Outdoors, a sheltered spot is best.

GOOD CHOICES: The species is the only one available.

Rubber Tree
Ficus elastica
MATURE HEIGHT × WIDTH: up to 6 feet × 4-5 feet
FLOWER COLORS: n/a
FLOWER SIZE: n/a
BLOOM TIME: n/a
SOIL: well-drained potting soil

From the jungles of Malaysia and India to the parlors of Victorian England, the rubber tree was among the first tropical plants to endear itself to gardeners. It remains popular to this day because it is so handsome and so easygoing.

The undersides of the thick, glossy green leaves are copper-colored and have a nice felted texture. The emergence of new foliage is interesting to watch—each one is curled and wrapped in thin, bright red tissue, a bit like a cigar. This protective covering eventually falls off as the leaf unfurls. If you happen to break off a leaf, milky white sap will ooze out; this was once used to make rubber until the sap of the Brazilian rubber tree proved superior.

For a good-looking specimen, indoors or out, give your rubber tree a decent, well-drained potting mix; bright but indirect light; and occasional water. Keep it out of drafts. Spider mites can be a problem, especially if you let the leaves get dusty, so polish them every few weeks.

GOOD CHOICES: 'Rubra'; 'Decora' ('Belgica').

Snake Plant, Mother-in-law's Tongue
Sansevieria trifasciata
MATURE HEIGHT × WIDTH: 3 feet × 1 inch
FLOWER COLORS: n/a
FLOWER SIZE: n/a
BLOOM TIME: n/a
SOIL: well-drained, sandy potting soil

Something of a curiosity, this extremely tough and tolerant houseplant is all leaf. There are stems, but they are under the soil surface. The tall spiky leaf pokes up and elongates, remaining only about an inch wide and attaining up to 3 feet or so in height. It may twist ever so slightly, a quality that has led some to compare the plant's appearance to an underwater plant moving with the current. Others think it looks like an undulating snake.

If a pot has more than one leaf, what you actually have is a cluster of close-growing plants, probably united by a tangle of underground stems. Because of the vertical nature of these leaves, a sturdy pot may be a good idea so that there's no danger of toppling over.

Dry air, sparing water, sandy potting soil, and any light conditions will suit this adaptable native of arid Africa. Situate pots on ascending shelves or steps, or behind flowering houseplants.

GOOD CHOICES: 'Laurentii' has cream-striped leaves.

Spider Plant
Chlorophytum comosum (capense)
MATURE HEIGHT × WIDTH: 1-3 feet × 1-3 feet
FLOWER COLORS: white
FLOWER SIZE: $^1/_2$ inch or less
BLOOM TIME: in warm weather
SOIL: well-drained potting soil

The big draw for this carefree plant is the fact that it generates all those "babies." A flurry of these around a "mother plant" apparently reminded someone of little airplanes buzzing around a big jet, leading to another, whimsical common name, "airplane plant."

This vigorous-growing, vivacious favorite is a sure bet for hanging baskets or any elevated spot where the plantlet-producing stems are able to hang down freely. Even dangling in the air, the plantlets begin developing roots and you can remove and pot up new young plants. Or scoot another pot near and let the roots grab on in the new home before severing its link to the mother plant. They also root easily in a cup of water.

The leaves, both on the main plant and on the little ones, are bladelike and only occasionally develop brown tips. If they do, try misting the plant occasionally to raise the humidity. White-striped ones show up better in lower-light locations such as the porch.

GOOD CHOICES: 'Variegatum' and 'Vittatum'.

Staghorn Fern
Platycerium species
MATURE HEIGHT × WIDTH: 3 feet × 3 feet
FLOWER COLORS: n/a
FLOWER SIZE: n/a
BLOOM TIME: n/a
SOIL: not needed; attach to support

In warm climates, or heated conservatories elsewhere, this spectacular plant is without peer. It makes an amazing, low-care decoration that everyone admires.

In nature, staghorn fern fastens itself to mature trees; gardeners can simply wire them to slabs of bark or tree-fern stems. Because the plant gets most of the moisture it needs from the air (technically it's an epiphyte), you don't need to worry much about water. If it looks dry, simply moisten its support and it will draw what it needs.

Fertilizing, even if there were an easy way to do it, is also unnecessary, for the flat, sterile fronds accumulate organic debris that helps feed it. The grayish-green fertile fronds are the attraction—those of a mature plant are forked, resembling deer or moose antlers.

A good way to display this unique plant is to rig its support to a big tree, fence, or lath wall. Semishade, as a patio or terrace area, is nice.

GOOD CHOICES: *Platycerium bifurcatum* is the smaller species; aptly named *P. grande* has gigantic, broad fertile fronds.

Wandering Jew

***Tradescantia fluminensis, T. albiflora,* and hybrids**

MATURE HEIGHT × WIDTH: trailing habit × 1-2 feet
FLOWER COLORS: white
FLOWER SIZE: inconspicuous
BLOOM TIME: rare, in warm weather
SOIL: well-drained potting soil

The evenly jointed stems do wander and branch, generating more foliage as they go. For this reason, it's best to grow this plant in a hanging basket or with its pot elevated, so the stems are free to spill down.

Unfortunately, as stems elongate, the leaves nearest the plant's crown tend to expire, so the plants quickly become leggy. Keep pinching them back. Alternatively, loop back the leafy part of a stem without breaking it and fasten it to the soil surface. As a last resort, cut off the offending stems right at the base; new growth will soon be generated.

If you do cut stems, you'll observe that they are semi-succulent. The high moisture content shows that this plant can survive periods of neglect. Only water when the soil surface is quite dry.

The regular species is green-leaved, but you may enjoy some of the colorful-leaved versions, which need more sun than the plain-leaved ones.

GOOD CHOICES: 'Variegata' has striped leaves; those of 'Rainbow' have white and pale lavender bands.

Wax Flower

Hoya carnosa

MATURE HEIGHT × WIDTH: 1-2 feet × trailing
FLOWER COLORS: white and pink
FLOWER SIZE: 1/2-inch clusters
BLOOM TIME: summer
SOIL: well-drained potting soil

Getting your hoya plant to flower is the challenge! Granted, this is a perfectly attractive foliage plant, with thick, 3-inch leaves that line trailing stems. There's usually a fairly long gap between individual leaves, so if it bothers you, tuck a support into the pot so the stems can wind and twine around for a fuller look.

There are a few tricks for getting those colorful, fragrant flower clusters to finally appear. Number one is your patience—most hoyas simply don't bloom until they are four or five years old. Potbound ones tend to flower easiest. Set the pot in a bright, sunny spot such as a west- or south-facing window or a patio table. Fertilize monthly during the warm months. Observing the dormant winter period is crucial: Bring the plants indoors, stop feeding, and reduce watering dramatically. Resume normal care in spring, and flower buds should form and open by summer. Do not remove the short stubs, because next year's little flower buds will form there.

GOOD CHOICES: 'Variegata' has leaves of green, pink, and creamy white.

Other indoor plants to try in containers:

- **Angelwing Begonia,** *Begonia* species and cultivars

- **Arboricola, Dwarf,** *Schefflera arboricola*

- **Asparagus Fern,** *Asparagus densiflorus* 'Sprengeri'

- **Bird's Nest Fern,** *Asplenium nidus* (top left)

- **Crown of Thorns,** *Euphorbia milii* var. *splendens* (top right)

- **Devil's Backbone,** *Pedilanthus tithymaloides*

- **Grape Ivy,** *Cissus rhombifolia*

- **New Zealand Flax,** *Phormium* species and hybrids

- **Norfolk Island Pine,** *Araucaria excelsa*

- **Peace Lily,** *Spathiphyllum* hyrids

- **Pencilbush,** *Euphorbia tirucalli*

- **Piggyback Plant,** *Tolmeia menziesii*

- **Weeping Fig,** *Ficus benjaminina* (center)

Perennials

Yes, you usually see perennials growing in the ground, in beds, and borders. But perhaps you would like to enjoy some up close, an intimacy that container culture allows. Or perhaps you don't have the space, and pots are your only or best chance to enjoy perennials.

Whatever the reason, rest assured that many perennials take well to the confines of a pot. In fact, they may even look better under closer care. You may be more apt to deadhead when you pass by a perennial every day. Their form may even be better, partly because of the extra attention you are able to lavish, but also because they are living in a less-competitive setting and will not have their stems pushed or crowded by neighboring plants.

Just as with perennials in a traditional garden, however, good soil and sufficient water is very important. Pot-grown perennials also benefit from regular doses of fertilizer to nourish their greedy root systems and thereby get the best possible display of foliage and, of course, flowers.

Though you may be tempted to snip off blooming flowers or even entire flower stalks from your pot-grown perennials, you may also hesitate, not wishing to decimate your display. Do it anyway! Perennials will finish up and go to seed, and if you let them, the flower show is over. Clip to be tidy or clip for bouquets, and the show should go on.

Not all perennials like life in a pot. Ones that form taproots simply don't get enough space, for instance, and of course really big, rambling ones are probably best passed by. Others have too brief a flowering period to justify your potting and nurturing efforts—Oriental poppies, for example. Below, however, is a list of excellent perennials that should do well. Get somewhat deeper, wider pots than you would for annuals or herbs, use a good fertile potting mix, and enjoy!

Aster, Perennial, Michaelmas Daisy
Aster nova-angliae, Aster nova-belgii,
Aster dumosus
MATURE HEIGHT × WIDTH: 1-6 feet × 2-4 feet
FLOWER COLORS: white, pink, lavender, purple, red
FLOWER SIZE: 1-3 inches
BLOOM TIME: late summer to fall
SOIL: well drained
ZONES: 4-8

This is a great group of late-season bloomers, indispensable for splendid color at this time of year. Bushy and sturdy, the asters were originally studded with tiny daisies of white, pale blue, or pink, until the hybridizers got hold of them. Ironically, this native American plant got the most attention overseas, particularly from English and German plant breeders (hence the British common name, Michaelmas daisy, which refers to a mid-September holiday). Now the flowers are bigger and more vividly colored. There are rosy pinks and rich purples, as well as excellent whites.

Normally, perennial asters are fairly big plants. You can certainly display them in something larger, such as half whiskey barrels. But you can also enjoy a number of fine dwarf varieties in smaller pots—these also tend to have more of a mounding habit, which looks good in containers.

GOOD CHOICES: Best dwarf cultivars: 'Purple Dome', lavender-blue 'Professor Anton Kippenberg', and white 'Schneekissen'.

Astilbe
Astilbe hybrids and cultivars
MATURE HEIGHT × WIDTH: 1½ to 4 feet × 1½ to 2½ feet
FLOWER COLORS: white, pink, lavender, red
FLOWER SIZE: 12- to 18-inch plumes
BLOOM TIME: varies
SOIL: fertile, moist, well drained
ZONES: 3-8

A favorite plant for shade gardeners, the lovely astilbe is also a good container plant when you wish to set up pots in a dim area. A few in a bigger pot, or several in individual pots gathered together, can really light up a dim area such as a north-facing deck or a shaded spot under an overhang. Their main requirements are a good, fertile soil mix and regular waterings.

Astilbe is one of those plants that looks good when viewed from all angles. The magnificent feathery plumes—actually masses of tiny flowers—rise up from the middle of the plant and come in a range of colors, from white to lavender to pink to red. Bloom times vary, so do a little homework in advance to target the bloom time you want. After the blooms finally fade, the somewhat ferny, toothed leaflets look truly handsome for the rest of the season.

GOOD CHOICES: Light pink 'Sprite' was the 1994 PPA Plant of the Year.

Bellflower
Campanula carpatica
MATURE HEIGHT × WIDTH: 6 inches × 6 inches
FLOWER COLORS: blue, white
FLOWER SIZE: 2-3 inches
BLOOM TIME: early to midsummer
SOIL: well drained
ZONES: 3-8

One species of bellflower is ideal for pot displays: little, mound-forming *Campanula carpatica*. Set in the middle of a pot, it forms a plant worth admiring from all sides. The medium-green leaves are attractive and not too dense, and the perky flowers rise above them on graceful little bare stalks. If you deadhead, the plants will be amazingly productive, making this a plant you can really depend on.

This bellflower comes in blue or white. Each looks excellent all on its own in a pot, or you can combine them. Alternatively, add either color to a larger, mixed container to create sort of a miniature cottage garden look. This is not an aggressive plant, and it will gladly share a stage with, say, violets, a miniature rosebush, or white lilies.

The soil mix should be moderately fertile and well drained. Don't let it get either soggy or too dry. Keep a lookout for slugs and snails, which relish campanulas—hopefully, your pot-grown ones will be out of range.

GOOD CHOICES: 'Blue Clips' and 'White Clips'.

Black-eyed Susan, Gloriosa Daisy
Rudbeckia species and cultivars
MATURE HEIGHT × WIDTH: 1-3 feet × 1-3 feet
FLOWER COLORS: yellow
FLOWER SIZE: 3-5 inches
BLOOM TIME: midsummer to fall
SOIL: average, well drained
ZONES: 3-8

Brilliant black-eyed Susans are among the easiest and longest lasting of all garden perennials, and container gardeners can also enjoy them; just either use a bigger pot or grow a shorter form. Give the plants a decent, well-drained soil mix and don't neglect watering, especially during hot spells.

All start blooming in midsummer and keep going until the cold weather of autumn finally slows them down. The clumps have handsome, dark green leaves that are untroubled by pests and diseases, and sturdy erect flower stems show off terrific golden daisies with dark centers. (The flowers also make excellent, long-lasting cut flowers and even hold their bright color when dried.)

The best one is widely acknowledged to be taller, prolific 'Goldsturm', but softer-yellow ones are available. Recent years have seen a flurry of fast-growing black-eyed Susans that are often treated like annuals, mostly selections of *R. hirta*.

GOOD CHOICES: 'Goldsturm', the 1999 PPA winner; *R. hirta* 'Indian Summer' won an AAS award in 1995; the 2003 AAS winner, 'Prairie Sun'.

Catmint
Nepeta × faassenii
MATURE HEIGHT × WIDTH: 1-1½ feet × 1½ feet
FLOWER COLORS: shades of purple, white
FLOWER SIZE: ½ inch, carried in loose racemes
BLOOM TIME: early to midsummer
SOIL: well drained
ZONES: 4-9

Masses of excellent purple flowers are guaranteed with this vigorous, clump-forming perennial. A member of the mint family, it has the aromatic leaves you'd expect, though they are not dark green but rather silvery gray-green. They make a beautiful backdrop for the lush flower show, which starts in early summer and carries on for many long weeks. Its modest size and manageable habit make it a fine choice for pots. Try it with some yellow flowers tucked in alongside, such as yarrow or coreopsis.

Average, well-drained soil is just fine—but do make sure that the container has a drainage hole or holes in the bottom. A spot in full sun is ideal, although catmint doesn't mind some afternoon shade. When flowering finally tapers off, trim back the plants to keep them compact and, often, to induce a second round of flowers.

GOOD CHOICES: The deep lavender flowers of 'Dropmore' are large and showy; 'Snowflake' is a white version.

Coral Bells
Heuchera species and cultivars
MATURE HEIGHT × WIDTH: 1 foot × 1 foot
FLOWER COLORS: pink, red, white
FLOWER SIZE: delicate bells, carried on leafless stalks
BLOOM TIME: spring to summer
SOIL: well drained
ZONES: 3-9

Got a shady deck, patio, or balcony? Display this plant in a pot and you can have it all: stunning foliage and attractive flowers. The durable, beautiful leaves are produced in mannerly clumps, and look a bit like those of ivy, though more rounded. They remain good-looking all season long. Slender little wands of delicate flowers (on close inspection, they're shaped like tiny bells) arise in late spring or early summer and add color and grace to the display. Some people even like to clip them for pretty filler in bouquets.

But these days the leaves have become the big attraction. Hybridizers have generated a flurry of new coral bells. Now there are selections whose foliage is bronze, russet, silvery, or that have these colors on their veins only for a rich, tapestry-like appearance. The names are mouthwatering as the plants.

GOOD CHOICES: 'Amethyst Mist', 'Cappuccino', 'Cathedral Windows', 'Chocolate Ruffles', 'Palace Purple' (1991 PPA award-winner), and 'Plum Pudding'—just to name a few!

Coreopsis
Coreopsis species and cultivars
MATURE HEIGHT × WIDTH: 1-3 feet × 2-3 feet
FLOWER COLORS: shades of yellow, pink
FLOWER SIZE: 1-3 inches
BLOOM TIME: summer
SOIL: well drained
ZONES: 5-9

Free-flowering coreopsis is perfect for a busy person; all you have to do is plunk a potful in a sunny spot. Coreopsis tolerates some neglect and prospers in hot, sunny weather. It has a rather open growth habit and fine-textured foliage, so if you grow it alone, you might do best to display in a somewhat larger or rustic-looking container that suits its casual demeanor. Otherwise, so you can easily add other plants to the same pot display for a fuller look.

The superb *C. verticillata* 'Moonbeam', with small daisies of soft lemon yellow, is probably the most versatile and goes with most every flower color. Some of the brighter-yellow coreopsis plants are best with other bold colors, particularly the double ones. Try these with any number of red, purple, or blue-flowered annuals. If you can find one, a pink-flowered coreopsis is a pretty, easygoing anchor for a pastel-themed pot.

GOOD CHOICES: 'Moonbeam', the PPA Plant of the Year in 1992; 'Early Sunrise' won an AAS award in 1989; dwarf 'Zagreb' pink; 'Sweet Dreams'.

Cranesbill Geranium, Hardy Geranium
Geranium species and hybrids
MATURE HEIGHT × WIDTH: 1-2 feet × 1-2 feet
FLOWER COLORS: shades of purple, blue, pink, white
FLOWER SIZE: 1-3 inches
BLOOM TIME: varies; spring or summer
SOIL: well drained
ZONES: 5-9

Some of the prettiest perennials belong to this broad and charming group, and any and all of them are fine choices for container culture. Most are low mounding plants or groundcovers, so they stay well in bounds.

Lovely, saucer-shaped flowers adorn these plants in late spring or on into summer. They come in various shades of purple and blue, as well as soft pink, bright pink, magenta, and white. The foliage is generally palm-shaped but lobed or deeply divided. The leaves of some hardy geraniums turn red or orange in the fall.

To look their best and to flower well, hardy geraniums like to have a decent, well-drained soil mix (container drainage holes are a must). Some like it a little moister while some tolerate drought—if you check on your plants regularly, you'll be able to get into a watering routine. Full sun is fine, but partial shade is often tolerated.

GOOD CHOICES: Old favorite 'Johnson's Blue'; 'Jolly Bee'; 'Ann Folkard'; 'Rozanne'.

Daylily
Hemerocallis cultivars
MATURE HEIGHT × WIDTH: 1-3 feet × 1-3 feet
FLOWER COLORS: every color except blue; also bicolors
FLOWER SIZE: 3-7 inches, depending on the cultivar
BLOOM TIME: summer
SOIL: fertile, well drained
ZONES: 3-10

Ever-popular daylilies are an absolute must for anyone who wants plenty of easygoing color all summer long. Regular-size daylilies, of course, will have to be placed in large tubs or planter boxes so they have sufficient space. But even better might be to grow some of the many dwarf daylilies; these are identical to the large ones, but have proportionally smaller blossoms and leaves.

To look their best, daylilies must have plenty of sunshine. A decent, well-drained soil mix is good, and for maximum flower production, fertilize the plants every few weeks. Regular, even watering is very important—a perennial as productive as the daylily cannot remain in bloom unless its roots and flowers have ample, consistent water.

By the way, it's true: Individual flowers only last for a day. It's just that the plants are so generous with their flowering that you don't always notice.

GOOD CHOICES: 'Stella d'Oro'; 'Happy Returns'; and 'Little Grapette'. For more, browse the offerings of any daylily specialist.

Dianthus, Pinks
Dianthus species and cultivars
MATURE HEIGHT × WIDTH: 6-12 inches × 12 inches
FLOWER COLORS: white, pink, red
FLOWER SIZE: 1-2 inches
BLOOM TIME: late spring to midsummer
SOIL: moist, well drained
ZONES: 3-8

Jaunty, spicy-scented dianthus flowers look just like tiny carnations, which, in effect, is exactly what they are. Usually seen in pink, red, and white, they're great for containers. They tend to form tidy little mats or mounds of thin, almost needlelike gray-green or blue-green foliage. Peak bloom is early in the season, but they'll keep pumping out more flowers if you pick bouquets or deadhead regularly.

Excellent drainage is a requirement. Surround their bases with gravel rather than organic mulch. And because dianthus plants like to grow in a slightly alkaline medium, sprinkle a few lime chips in the pot at the beginning of the season. Problems with pests and diseases are blessedly rare. Full sun brings out their best.

Array dianthus plants of the same or varying colors together, or mix them—pink ones with green foliage plants, purple-hued ones with lavender or catmint, and crimson ones at the feet of white lilies.

GOOD CHOICES: *D. gratianopolitanus* 'Bath's Pink'; *D. deltoides* 'Zing Rose'; 'Betty Morton'; and 'Snowbank'.

Hosta
Hosta species and cultivars
MATURE HEIGHT × **WIDTH:** varies
FLOWER COLORS: white or lavender
FLOWER SIZE: varies; blooms are carried on stalks
BLOOM TIME: varies
SOIL: fertile, well drained
ZONES: 3-9

Granted, the sprawling hostas with the massive leaves are not meant for container culture, but you can certainly enjoy success with many of the smaller ones. Indeed, the attractive form of this classic shade plant is well suited to display in a pot.

So focus your search on the smaller ones before you fall in love with a certain leaf texture or color. For a shady spot, you'd do well to seek out a gold or white-rimmed or splashed hosta that'll show up better. While all hostas are considered foliage plants, they do flower, and the flowers can be very appealing. In early, mid-, or late summer, depending on the variety, these rise above the clump of leaves on arching stalks.

To inspire your pot-grown hostas to be healthy and to flower, give them fertile but well-drained soil mix, and feed them monthly. Keep them cool or the foliage will suffer.

GOOD CHOICES: The American Hosta Society gives out annual awards, so look for winners. Two superb dwarf hostas: 'Blue Cadet' and 'Pandora's Box'.

Japanese Blood Grass
Imperata cylindrica
MATURE HEIGHT × **WIDTH:** 12-24 inches × 18-24 inches
FLOWER COLORS: silvery
FLOWER SIZE: 8-inch spikelets
BLOOM TIME: summer
SOIL: average, well drained
ZONES: 5-9

Since the boom in ornamental grasses in the recent past, horticulturists have winnowed out certain ones that are genuinely garden-worthy. Alas, many are very big plants, while others are invasive. Your best bet with the best ones, including Japanese Blood Grass, is to grow them in pots.

A modest-sized grass of remarkable beauty, Japanese Blood Grass is prized for its unique foliage. The blades are broad and flat, and the coloration begins green at the bases but segues to a striking blood red from the middle on up to the tip-top. It is spectacular when backlit by the sun, so be sure to place your pot strategically. For extra drama, grow it in a decorative pot. For dashing horticultural drama, include it in a mixed container with yellow, purple, or orange flowers. (Its own flowers don't always appear and aren't that spectacular anyway.)

As for care, ordinary soil mix is fine, fertilizing is not necessary, and regular watering is sufficient in most locations.

GOOD CHOICES: The mostly widely available cultivar, 'Red Baron'.

Japanese Painted Fern
Athyrium niponicum (goeringianum) 'Pictum'
MATURE HEIGHT × **WIDTH:** 1-2 feet × 1 foot
FLOWER COLORS: Foliage plant
FLOWER SIZE: n/a
BLOOM TIME: n/a
SOIL: fertile, well drained
ZONES: 5-8

Lady's Mantle
Alchemilla mollis
MATURE HEIGHT × **WIDTH:** 1-2 feet × 1-2 feet
FLOWER COLORS: chartreuse
FLOWER SIZE: tiny clusters carried in loose sprays
BLOOM TIME: late spring to early summer
SOIL: moist, well drained
ZONES: 4-8

Easily the most popular cultivated fern, Japanese painted fern is great for containers. It's not too large, and its unique fronds are not the same old green, but pewtery-silver with a green border; the veins and stems are plum or wine-red. Best situated in a shady spot, a little extra sunlight can inspire more intense coloring. Experiment with this by moving the pot around to different locations and waiting to see what happens.

This fern's weeping habit is ideal for a pot with an Oriental pattern—if the design is not too ornate or the color wrong for the silvery fronds. The growing medium is important; instead of a light potting mix, fill the pot with organically rich soil. And never neglect watering.

The most compatible plants for Japanese painted fern are other shade-lovers: Astilbe and coral bells, and in a bigger pot, a dwarf Japanese maple.

GOOD CHOICES: The original received the PPA 2004 Plant of the Year award. Newcomer 'Red Beauty' has especially bright red stems and veins.

This perennial has a certain elegance that lends itself very well to display in a container—but not just any container. For this you will want an urn. Filled with fertile, well-drained soil mix and with lady's mangle held aloft, this conjures an enchanting British Cotswolds garden. You almost want to put on your Wellington boots and go out to admire it as the morning dew is drying.

Actually you won't want to miss the morning dew: The felted, scalloped leaves of this mounding plant collect droplets of water that bead up like quicksilver.

Lady's mantle also has pretty flowers. They rise above the leaves in late spring or early summer on slender, branched stalks. Their unusual chartreuse color makes a sharp contrast with the leaves. Flower arrangers delight in tucking them in mixed bouquets of much larger, colorful flowers. On the plant and in the urn, they froth over the lovely leaves in a delightful way.

GOOD CHOICES: There are no cultivars, but another worthy species is *A. erythropoda*.

Shasta Daisy
Leucanthemum × *superbum*

MATURE HEIGHT × WIDTH: 1-3^1/$_2$ feet × 2-3 feet
FLOWER COLORS: white
FLOWER SIZE: 2-3 inches
BLOOM TIME: summer
SOIL: fertile, moist, well drained
ZONES: 5-9

Here's the best and brightest classic daisy going. If you keep it watered and deadheaded, its output of perky flowers is incredible. The plant itself can get big, so display it in a substantial pot such as a half-barrel, or try a dwarf variety. Frilly or "double" flowered versions look more like mums than daisies, but for sheer spunk, the regular flower is hard to beat.

This is a sun-lover, so site it in a bright, prominent spot. Two pots flanking an entryway or a series of pots on the side of the steps leading to a door are both great ways to use potted daisies. This is even truer if your house is a bright color that contrasts with the daisies.

Good drainage is important, as damp roots lead to rot. Start with a decent, lighter soil mix, make sure your container has drainage holes, and don't overwater.

GOOD CHOICES: Heat-tolerant 'Becky' was the PPA Plant of the Year in 2003; good dwarf versions include 'Little Princess', 'Miss Muffet', and 'Silver Princess'.

Willow Leaf Mexican Petunia
Ruellia brittoniana

MATURE HEIGHT × WIDTH: 2-4 feet × sprawling
FLOWER COLORS: lavender
FLOWER SIZE: 1-2 inches
BLOOM TIME: mid- to late summer
SOIL: average, well drained
ZONES: 6-9

A native Southwestern wildflower, this beauty is tough. It has pink, purple, or white, petunia-like flowers and remains in bloom for most of the summer. Once established, even baking hot sun doesn't daunt it. It also prospers in bright shade, on, say, a front porch.

It is a bit of a rambler and a sprawler, so enterprising gardeners have found it to be better in a pot than in the ground. In a pot, it still flowers exuberantly, and the stems spill over the sides. For best results, water the plants regularly while still young. As the summer wears on, they'll become more drought tolerant.

Ruellia is a nice mixer with other sun-lovers that also have an informal nature, such as coreopsis. It would also be fun to pair it with larger-flowered, color-matched (or contrasted!) petunias.

GOOD CHOICES: There seems to be some nomenclatural confusion with this plant—*R. caroliniensis* and *R. cilosa* are also offered at native-plant nurseries and seem to be either very similar to or the same as *R. humilis*.

Other perennials to try in containers:

- **Basket-of-Gold,** *Aurinia saxatalis*
- **Bergenia,** *Bergenia cordifolia*
- **Candytuft,** *Iberis sempervirens* (top left)
- **Hollyhock Mallow,** *Malva alcea* (top right)
- **Lamb's Ears,** *Stachys byzantina*
- **Primrose,** *Primula* species and cultivars

- **Purple Heart,** *Setcreasea pallida*
- **Sedum,** *Sedum* species, hybrids, and cultivars
- **Spike Speedwell,** *Veronica spicata*
- **Violet,** *Viola* species and cultivars (center)
- **Yarrow,** *Achillea filipendulina*

Shrubs and Trees

a tree or a shrub displayed in a pot is a major garden decision—and investment. It can certainly be done, and the result can be quite impressive, but you need to be practical. Even smaller candidates are going to require a substantial pot to accommodate their root systems. A larger pot may help buffer those roots from winter cold, though it's foolish to plant a tree or shrub that you know is not hardy in your climate. Winter protection measures can always be taken, of course, including wrapping the entire affair, pot, plant, and all, or dragging the heavy container indoors for the coldest months, but don't set yourself up for a constant struggle. Instead, choose a handsome plant that is suitable for your climate.

The other consideration after cold hardiness is placement. As in a regular garden, any tree or shrub takes up major space and ideally you should find a spot for it before other, smaller plants or even patio furniture and garden ornaments are placed in the vicinity.

Potted trees and shrubs need loving attention, especially in their early years. Water must not be neglected, and fertilizing during the growing season will inspire better foliage and flowering. Pruning and shaping are very important, because a plant that gets too big or full could overwhelm its container, and its roots will not be able to nourish it sufficiently. Make life easier by selecting naturally smaller and slower-growing selections. Here are some fine choices. Note that while they may grow larger out in the ground, the same or similar trees are always a smaller size in a container, as the container helps control growth.

Bay, Sweet
Laurus nobilis
MATURE HEIGHT × WIDTH: 6-12 feet × 1-3 feet
FLOWER COLORS: yellow
FLOWER SIZE: small, in clusters
BLOOM TIME: spring to summer
SOIL: well-drained potting soil
ZONES: 8-11

A classic formal container plant, the lovely bay tree can be kept to a manageable size in a large pot. It has a naturally compact habit, and grows rather slowly. Unless you prune it otherwise, it develops into a broad-based, multi-stemmed plant.

The leaves are the reason to grow it—they're oval, up to 4 inches long, and sweetly aromatic (indeed, you can, and should, pinch some off for use in cooking!). It may flower, depending on its age and whether it gets enough sunlight. If it does, you can expect clusters of small yellow flowers that draw bees. Small black or dark purple berries follow.

For best results, grow your bay tree in a pot of well-drained soil (it must have a drainage hole!). Don't overwater. If it's outside, it will appreciate some shelter from the blazing midsummer sun. It responds well to clipping and shaping and is often trained as a standard; indeed, you can buy it that way.

GOOD CHOICES: 'Saratoga' has a more treelike habit than the species.

Boxwood
Buxus sempervirens
MATURE HEIGHT × WIDTH: 2-3 feet × 2-3 feet (dwarf)
FLOWER COLORS: creamy white
FLOWER SIZE: tiny, in clusters
BLOOM TIME: spring
SOIL: well-drained potting soil
ZONES: 6-8

The favorite use of potted boxwood plants is in urns or other formal containers, placed at intervals astride a driveway or entryway, or around a formal reflecting pool. They lend themselves to these uses because their dark green foliage is easily clipped into neat shapes.

However, boxwood is not very cold hardy. When grown in the ground, chilly winters can brown the leaves or outright kill the bushes. Container-grown ones are even more vulnerable: A smaller pot could dry out and freeze solid. So if cold hardiness is an issue, be prepared to take protection measures, perhaps moving them inside for the winter months. In mild climates, of course, potted boxwoods should look grand practically year-round.

Choose a naturally dwarf variety and grow it in a lighter soil mix that drains well. Pots are a viable choice for Southern gardeners simply because heavy clay garden soil makes boxwood miserable, plus root-knot nematodes can be a issue.

GOOD CHOICES: There are a number of good dwarf varieties. The most common is 'Vardar Valley'.

Camellia
Camellia japonica
MATURE HEIGHT × WIDTH: 1-3 feet × 1-3 feet
FLOWER COLORS: red, pink, white
FLOWER SIZE:
BLOOM TIME: late winter to spring
SOIL: well-drained potting soil
ZONES: 7-8

Though normally a rambling bush that prospers in mild climates, camellia is also practical as a potted plant. Once the darling of Victorian gardeners, its popularity continues unabated to this day because the flowering show is so generous and the glossy dark-green leaves are so handsome. The show arrives early, too: a great way to usher in spring.

The soil mix is the key to success. It should be moist, well drained, and somewhat acidic. Be sure the pot, tub, or urn has a drainage hole, for standing water is disastrous. Full-on sun dries out the pots too quickly, plus bleaches out or shortens the life of the flowers. Your best bet is to display your potted camellias on a semi-shady porch or under the shelter of a pergola or lath house.

The flowers are surprisingly durable and wonderfully colorful, and if your plants are happy, they'll be very prolific. You may even pick off a few blossoms and float them in a bowl of water indoors.

GOOD CHOICES: Just pick from dozens of colors!

Dwarf Conifers
Various species and cultivars
MATURE HEIGHT × WIDTH: usually 1-4 feet × 1-4 feet
FLOWER COLORS: n/a
FLOWER SIZE: n/a
BLOOM TIME: n/a
SOIL: well-drained potting soil
ZONES: varies from Zones 4-8

Ever-popular dwarf conifers make excellent accent plants for today's smaller gardens. They can be displayed solo, or arrayed formally in a row, even to the point of forming a privacy screen. They tend to be tough, growing slowly and remaining handsome year-round, and are rarely ever prey to pests or in need of substantial clipping or pruning.

Generally speaking, potted conifers have the same basic requirements. They need a sturdy, heavy pot so that they will not topple over in wind. The pot should also have drainage holes, as "wet feet" tend to be detrimental; the soil mix should be fertile and well drained. Full-on sunshine dries them out quickly, and because some are shallow rooted, a moisture-conserving mulch of bark chips on the soil surface is a good idea.

GOOD CHOICES: A nursery will offer a range of small ones, from arborvitaes to cedars to cypresses to the ubiquitous dwarf Alberta spruce (*Picea glauca* 'Conica'). Pre-shaped or topiary forms are often available.

Gardenia
Gardenia jasminoides
MATURE HEIGHT × WIDTH: 2-4 feet × 2-4 feet
FLOWER COLORS: white
FLOWER SIZE: 2-3 inches
BLOOM TIME: late spring to fall, depending on cultivar
SOIL: well-drained potting soil
ZONES: 8-10

Floridians may get to enjoy big, blowsy gardenia bushes in the ground, but the rest of us must settle for potted plants. Luckily, gardenias like pot culture. The glossy green leaves are fabulous, and the flowers are some of the most gorgeous, headily fragrant beauties you could hope to grow. Depending on the cultivar, they may bloom around Easter or well into the summer months.

Pot your gardenia in an organically rich mix and fertilize constantly during the growing season with an acidic plant food. In return, the plant will explode with those wonderful blooms. Clip off spent ones right away to prolong the show.

After flowering is over, clip back overly eager new growth to maintain its shape. If white flies or aphids appear, combat them aggressively, first with sprays of water and, if needed, with insecticidal soap applied according to label directions. Finally, if your winters are chilly, try overwintering the pot in a cool room indoors (give it indirect light and water only occasionally).

GOOD CHOICES: 'White Gem'.

Gold Dust Plant
Aucuba japonica
MATURE HEIGHT × WIDTH: 4-6 feet × 3-4 feet
FLOWER COLORS: maroon
FLOWER SIZE: tiny
BLOOM TIME: spring; rare
SOIL: well-drained potting soil
ZONES: 7-10

This handsome plant prefers cooler locations and tolerates low light. So a container can be placed in a dim room or hallway—or outdoors on an east- or west-facing porch, or even under the shelter of a tall shade tree in the yard. Drafts and breezes don't seem to harm it, which can't be said of some other containerized trees. However, it does need good potting soil, a container with a drainage hole, and regular but sparing water throughout the warm months.

You can always count on this plant to be lush with shiny leaves; the species is plain green and the cultivar 'Variegata' is speckled and dusted with gold marks. The form is nice and full, almost shrubby. The flowers are inconspicuous and the issue is further complicated by the fact that, like holly bushes, the plants are either male or female; a female plant grown near a male plant will develop bright red berries in the fall and winter months. But the main draw remains the beautiful foliage.

GOOD CHOICES: 'Nana' and 'Variegata'.

Japanese Maples
Acer japonicum, *Acer palmatum,* **and others**
MATURE HEIGHT × **WIDTH: 3-6 feet** × **3-6 feet**
FLOWER COLORS: red to purple
FLOWER SIZE: 1/2-1 inch
BLOOM TIME: spring
SOIL: well-drained potting soil
ZONES: 5-9

Long popular in Japan as bonsai, Japanese maples are excellent for pots. Just choose a cultivar billed as "dwarf" or even "semi-dwarf." This may still mean several feet high and wide. The tree will look excellent in a big tub where it gets some shelter from very hot sun and drying winds.

Be careful because too much sun can scorch the leaves. If you have the choice, give your potted maple morning sun and afternoon shade. Beware of reflected light, which can lead to burnt leaf edges in very hot summer weather.

Keep the potting mix evenly moist but not soggy. Consistent watering should do the trick—and be sure the pot, no matter how big, has a drainage hole. Fertilize lightly during the spring and summer to see if it boosts leaf health and color. Every few years you may need to repot your small tree to a slightly larger pot; undertake this project in spring, when growth is just starting.

GOOD CHOICES: 'Red Pygmy'; 'Elegans'; and 'Shigure Bato'.

Rose, Miniature
Rosa **cultivars**
MATURE HEIGHT × **WIDTH: 1-3 feet** × **1-3 feet**
FLOWER COLORS: many
FLOWER SIZE: 1-3 inches
BLOOM TIME: summer
SOIL: well-drained potting soil
ZONES: 6-9

Container gardeners do not have to deny themselves the pleasures of raising beautiful roses. A huge array of miniature rose varieties is now available. Choose the colors you like, because care and culture is pretty much the same in all cases.

The secret to excellent potted mini-roses is a decent soil mix in a sturdy pot with drainage holes and regular watering. Because the soil mix gets depleted of its nutrients over time, you'd be wise to fertilize regularly in spring and summer. Since they bloom so enthusiastically and for so long, mini-roses add color to your container displays. Tuck pots among foliage plants, or add a mini-rose to a mixed planting.

Unlike many big rosebushes, minis are grown on their own roots (they are not grafted). So if the branches get harmed or cold damaged, new growth will still be the same as what you expect.

GOOD CHOICES: There are hundreds of mini varieties! American Rose Society award-winners are a good place to start. Or try 'Child's Play' or 'Rise'n'Shine'.

Other shrubs and trees to try in containers (always seek out dwarf or small cultivars):

- **Abelia,** *Abelia × grandiflora*
- **Arborvitae,** *Thuja occidentalis*
- **Deutzia,** *Deutzia* species and cultivars (top left)
- **Heavenly Bamboo,** *Nandina domestica*
- **Hydrangea,** *Hydrangea* species and cultivars (top right)
- **Japanese Cedar,** *Cryptomeria japonica*
- **Loropetalum,** *Loropetalum chinense*
- **Spirea,** *Spiraea* species and cultivars (center)
- **Weigela,** *Weigela florida* cultivars
- **Wintercreeper,** *Euonymus fortunei*
- **Yellow Sage,** *Lantana camara* and cultivars

Tropicals

There is a small but tacit difference between plants from the tropics that have traditionally been grown indoors as "potted" plants, and those tropical beauties that are used solely for their bold foliage or flowers as temporary outdoor accents. The trend toward using tropicals almost like big annuals (or cut back and kept over the winter for another shot outdoors the next summer) is gathering steam.

Truthfully, many of these plants are either too big, or too fussy, to keep indoors all year. They are often hard to come by, or expensive, but the flair they add to the spring, summer, and fall garden—and even indoors over the winter, where there is space—is undeniable. Who can say no to exotic bird-of-paradise, giant elephant ears, banana trees, homegrown lemons, and anything named "jungle flame"?

In general, such plants are technically perennials or even shrubs or small trees in the tropics, but when they are put in a container and used as seasonal accents around a pool or patio, they tend to stay smaller than their wild cousins. Regular fertilization and watering, with occasional pruning to keep them in bounds, are about all they need.

Except, of course, for dragging them in for the winter, or back out in the spring.

Angel Trumpet
Brugmansia species
MATURE HEIGHT × WIDTH: 6-8 feet × 4-6 feet
FLOWER COLORS: White, peach, yellow, orange, purple
FLOWER SIZE: trumpets to 12 inches long
BLOOM TIME: summer and fall
SOIL: any well-drained, moist potting soil

There are two main kinds of angel trumpets: the low-growing *Datura*, with white flowers, and the richly hybridized *Brugmansias*, which in general are small trees with large trumpet flowers. Both are exotic, interesting conversation plants sure to bring comments.

The upright trees of *Brugmansia* have sparse branches covered with large, oval pointed leaves. Long, cigar-shaped twisted buds snap open fairly quickly at dusk into large, flaring, trumpet-shaped flowers. These are usually very fragrant and may attract large hawk moths. The seedpods that follow are interesting to behold, but bear in mind that the seeds within are poisonous.

A site with morning sun and protection from hot afternoon or radiated heat from a wall is ideal for this beautiful plant. Water regularly and feed lightly to keep plants flowering instead of just producing leaves. Prune after flowering, and root 1- to 2-foot-long stem sections in the fall, in a tall vase of only a few inches of water.

GOOD CHOICES: 'Charles Grimaldi'; 'Jamaica Yellow'; 'Ecuador Pink'; 'Peaches and Cream'; 'Cornucopia'.

Banana
Musa species
MATURE HEIGHT × WIDTH: 4-15 feet × 3-8 feet
FLOWER COLORS: Purple, yellow, crimson
FLOWER SIZE: Long, hanging clusters to 3 feet
BLOOM TIME: Summer of second year
SOIL: Very well drained, high in organic matter

Nothing says tropics more than bananas. Wind- and cold-resistant and dwarf varieties and those with colorful leaves and flowers make this a most interesting plant. Each grows from a slow-growing clump, with false trunks made of old leaf stalks, with new growth erupting from the center of each trunk. The huge, waxy-green, burgundy, or variegated leaves are long, wide blades.

Flowers are complicated-looking: Female flowers look like small bananas, with male pollinator flowers nearer the bottom, encased in a purple sheath. It takes a year and a half for a stem to mature enough to flower and make small bananas. A hard freeze may cause the loss of that year's fruit. Some gardeners cut their plants back severely and store them over the winter in cool garages or basements, then re-cut the leggy, pale winter growth by spring.

GOOD CHOICES: Dwarf Cavendish; 'Mysore' or "lady fingers;" 'Goldfinger'; 'Dwarf Brazilian'; 'Ice Cream' ('Blue Java'); 'Rojo'. Ornamental species (*M.* × *paradisiaca*, *M. ornata*, *M. velutina*, others).

Bird of Paradise
Strelitzia reginae
MATURE HEIGHT × WIDTH: 4-5 feet × 3-4 feet
FLOWER COLORS: range/blue/white
FLOWER SIZE: 6-10 inches
BLOOM TIME: all season in warm areas
SOIL: any well-drained potting soil

The exotic flowers on this drought-hardy plant almost look fake, and they last so long they might as well be made of plastic. The gaudy, long-stemmed blossoms, which look like pointed woodpecker silhouettes, are irresistible to floral arrangers.

Some of these seemingly indestructible plants have been hauled indoors and out with the seasons for generations. The plants flower best when tightly potbound, so there is no need to repot them. They do thrive on regular feedings, but will also tolerate a long drought with ease.

The stalked, leathery leaves, wide and waxy blue-green, resist damage from splashing water, making the plants very popular near poolside. Snip off faded leaves as needed to keep yours looking healthy and perky.

When it comes into bloom—more in cool weather than in summer—you will see why it has been cherished for so long.

GOOD CHOICES: *S. nicolai*, is called either "giant" or "white" bird of paradise; unless you have a really big tub, it may be hard to manage.

Bottlebrush
Callistemon species
MATURE HEIGHT × WIDTH: 5-8 feet × 4-5 feet
FLOWER COLORS: bright red or pale yellow
FLOWER SIZE: spikes to 6 inches
BLOOM TIME: spring through fall
SOIL: well-drained or even heavy, moist potting soil

Several species of bottlebrush are sold, but all can be massive. To grow one successfully in a container, not to mention keep it small enough to make bringing it indoors for the winter possible, the plant must be kept thinned and tip pruned.

Hummingbirds go nuts around these nearly ever-blooming sun plants. Flowering twigs are rigid and brittle, but recover quickly from pruning—unless you cut them back too hard, past where leaves are still on the stem.

The stems are surrounded with dense spikes of long, bristle-like stamens. Most are red, though some pale yellow. Woody beadlike seed capsules remain for many months, sometimes years, on old stems.

Generally found growing in moist areas of their native Australia, bottlebrush plants can tolerate waterlogged soils part of the year, making them ideal companions for elephant ears and Mexican petunia. They can also handle the splash of nearby water fountains, or the high humidity of a swimming-pool area.

GOOD CHOICES: Lemon bottlebrush (*C. citrinus*) and weeping bottlebrush (*C. viminalis*).

Bromeliads
Aechmea, Billbergia, numerous others
MATURE HEIGHT × **WIDTH: 4-18 inches × 3-24 inches**
FLOWER COLORS: every imaginable color
FLOWER SIZE: 2-12 inches
BLOOM TIME: during warm spells
SOIL: extremely well-drained bark-based potting soil

Members of the large "pineapple" family of plants, bromeliads are mostly stemless with clustered leaves, many of which are handsomely marked. Flower clusters often have colorful, long-lasting bracts. Most are epiphytes (grow in trees), while others are terrestrial (grow on the ground or well-drained potting soil). They are easily raised in containers. Array a collection together on a patio or deck, or (if shade tolerant) under the branches of a large yard tree.

Those that hold water in their central cups should not be kept wet indoors, or the water can stagnate and cause rot.

GOOD CHOICES: There are too many to even mention all the main types. However, the most popular include *Ananas comosus,* the familiar pineapple; *Aechmea,* with urn-like rosettes that can hold water; *Billbergia,* tall, urn-shaped epiphytes; *Cryptanthus* bromeliads, commonly called "earth stars;" *Neoregelia,* which grow as rosettes of stiff leaves; and some *Tillandsia,* with showy flowers.

Cigar Plant
Cuphea ignea
MATURE HEIGHT × **WIDTH: 2-4 feet × 2-3 feet**
FLOWER COLORS: red, yellow, peach
FLOWER SIZE: 3-inch tubular
BLOOM TIME: during warm weather
SOIL: well-drained potting mix

Compact yet airy, this long-blooming perennial from Mexico and Central America works well as a "filler." Its narrow, dark green leaves (up to an inch or so long) and spikes of flowers that peek out from showier foliage plants provide a nice touch between bold-textured plants and those with spiky foliage or flowers. Its bright flowers, each tipped with white and a small black ring (like a lit cigar with ash), are very attractive to hummingbirds.

Pinch growing tips throughout the spring, summer, and early fall to encourage bushiness and more flower stem production. Older plants can be cut back severely in the late fall or early winter, and they can sprout again well before time to set them back out in the spring. Cuttings are also fairly easy to root.

When growing cigar plant indoors, or near a hot area outside, cluster it with other tropicals to help provide the humidity it thrives on.

GOOD CHOICES: 'Lutea' and 'Petite Peach'. Relatives include Mexican Heather (*C. hyssopifolia*) and "bat face" (*C. llavea*).

Citrus
Citrus species
MATURE HEIGHT × WIDTH: 4-7 feet × 3-5 feet
FLOWER COLORS: white
FLOWER SIZE: 1-1^1/$_2$ inches wide
BLOOM TIME: spring and summer
SOIL: well-drained potting soil with extra sand

You can grow your own citrus—to some extent—in containers, just as Louis XIV did at Versailles. With occasional pruning to thin out tall or gangly growth, and light snipping of stem tips to encourage bushiness, several kinds of citrus are easy to keep growing.

Still, the small evergreen trees need space for air circulation and good drainage. Glossy oval leaves and thorny branches are typical, and all have very fragrant white flowers in the spring and summer, followed by sweet, juicy fruits of various sizes and flavors depending on species and variety.

Though calamondin and kumquats can stay in smaller pots for years, most do best in large containers, at least 1^1/$_2$ or 2 feet in diameter. Use a slow-release fertilizer to keep plants vigorous. Over the winter, keep your plants in a cool basement or garage and protect them from hard freezes.

GOOD CHOICES: Small-fruited kumquat and calamondin are the easiest; they flower freely and are kept compact with pruning. Mandarins, grapefruit, lime, lemon, Meyer lemon, and citron are also very popular.

Croton
Codiaeum variegatum
MATURE HEIGHT × WIDTH: 4-5 feet × 3 feet
FLOWER COLORS: not showy
FLOWER SIZE: n/a
BLOOM TIME: n/a
SOIL: well-drained potting soil

This is one of the most commonly grown plants by "garden variety" gardeners in the Tropics, especially in its native Africa, where the huge specimens by nearly every door can attain 8 to 10 feet or more and half as wide. When container grown, croton is usually kept to a single stem up to 3 or 4 feet tall. Its wavy, foot-long, leathery leaves, sometimes wide like a rubber tree or very narrow and curly, are glossy and splashed in every imaginable combination of green, yellow, orange, pink, purple, red, and bronze—the more sun, the more color.

If overwintering indoors, keep this humidity-loving plant out of a heater draft. The plants will also not tolerate cold—even a few cool nights outdoors can cause it to shed its leaves, if only temporarily. Keep it moist, not wet, and in a south or west window where it can get the most sun in the winter. Dust leaves occasionally. Spider mites and mealy bugs can be pests, but are easily controlled with insecticidal soap.

GOOD CHOICES: 'Spirale'; 'Andreanum'; 'Majesticum'; and 'Aureo-maculatum'.

Elephant Ears
Colocasia esculenta
MATURE HEIGHT × WIDTH: 3-5 feet × 2-4 feet
FLOWER COLORS: not showy
FLOWER SIZE: n/a
BLOOM TIME: n/a
SOIL: moist soils, tolerates heavy, sometimes wet soils

Big, bold foliage translates into a perfect complement for ferns and backdrop for other moisture-loving plants. They grow well in large pots, and can even be set in full sun if kept watered. They're also perfect where large, quick screening is needed from spring to fall.

Giant, heart-shaped green leaves grow on stalks up to four or more feet tall. This plant has a tendency to "run" in wet soils, almost to the point of being a pest (it is on the banned "invasive exotic plant" lists in some Southern states).

Elephant ears are surprisingly hardy outdoors, but die down in the winter to their root-like tubers. Their large leaves may need protection from strong winds.

The unusual, calla-like spathe flowers are hidden in foliage canopy. Most gardeners ignore them, or cut them off to promote new foliage production. To boost performance, feed these fast-growing foliage plants lightly but regularly, and keep their soil moist during hot spells.

GOOD CHOICES: 'Illustris'; 'Black Magic'; and 'Chicago Harlequin'. *Alocasia macrorrhiza* is the choice "upright" elephant ear.

Firespike, Scarlet Flame
Odontonema strictum
MATURE HEIGHT × WIDTH: 4-5 feet × 2-5 feet
FLOWER COLORS: fiery red
FLOWER SIZE: spikes up to a foot tall
BLOOM TIME: summer through fall
SOIL: any decent potting soil, even moist or heavy kinds

A showy summer and fall flowering plants for big containers, this Central America native is visited by butterflies and hummingbirds continuously, so site it where you can enjoy watching these visitors.

Without pruning, the multi-stemmed shrub can reach 5 or more feet tall and nearly as wide. Its oval, shiny, deep green leaves are up to 6 inches long. Leaves blacken quickly when exposed to frost, but the plant can be cut back and forced to sprout again indoors.

Foot-long spikes of bright red tubular flowers are produced above and contrast starkly against the glossy foliage from midsummer through fall, even in fairly dense shade, making it a good alternative to hosta where slugs are a problem. Interplant it with ferns, taller ginger lilies, and palms, where its broad leaves make a good contrast and its spikes of flowers can stand out.

Firespike is very easy to propagate from stem cuttings, especially in the summer and early fall.

GOOD CHOICES: Only the species is available.

Flowering Maple, Chinese Lantern
Abutilon species and hybrids
MATURE HEIGHT × WIDTH: 3-8 feet × 3-4 feet
FLOWER COLORS: white, yellow, pink, or red
FLOWER SIZE: 2-3 inches
BLOOM TIME: nearly continuously in warm weather
SOIL: any well-drained, moist soil of moderate fertility

Used from Victorian days as a "parlor" plant, this is widely considered to be one of the best hummingbird attractors around. There is a continuous production of drooping, bell-shaped flowers, 2 to 3 inches across and all but dripping with nectar.

Fast-growing, upright, arching stems up to 8 or more feet tall can be "pinched" for more bushy growth and to keep the plant compact enough to bring indoors in the winter. Leaves are broad and maplelike, 6 or more inches across, and are quite often speckled or variegated.

Pruning severely during indoors-outdoors transitions helps keep new growth forming and old leaves from shedding or burning around the edges from changes in the humidity (or lack of humidity). The stems are very easy to root, especially if you keep the humidity around cuttings high. Note: Too much nitrogen fertilizer forces leafy growth and fewer flowers.

GOOD CHOICES: 'Clementine'; 'Bartley Schwartz'; 'Marion Stewart'; 'Moonchimes'; and Brazilian maple (*A. pictum* 'Thomsonii').

Hawaiian Ti
Cordyline terminalis
MATURE HEIGHT × WIDTH: 4-6 feet × 3-5 feet
FLOWER COLORS: lavender or white
FLOWER SIZE: small, but in 2-foot clusters
BLOOM TIME: spring
SOIL: well-drained potting soil

This gaudy potted plant, a common souvenir from Hawaii often bought as a small "log," is almost too shocking to use effectively. A yucca relative, it has lush foliage that looks great near a swimming pool. Its long, pointed, lance-shaped leaves are wide for their length, and are usually streaked in red, yellow, magenta, or variegations.

Ti, which is sometimes sold erroneously as a type of dracaena, is often used as a showy understory planting where hot colors are needed or acceptable (it tolerates very low light), or as a specimen—it's one of the few plants that actually looks great in a chrome container.

The thin, bamboo-like stems are very easy to root. Those dried-out sections or "logs" can be laid in a well-drained but moist potting soil. New plants will grow at nearly every leaf joint with their own shoots and roots.

GOOD CHOICES: There are several named cultivars, but none are more notable than the others. A larger, hardier "giant dracaena" (*C. australis*) also has several very colorful cultivars.

Heliconia, Parrot Plant
Heliconia psittacorum
MATURE HEIGHT × WIDTH: 2-6 feet × spreading habit
FLOWER COLORS: many
FLOWER SIZE: stalks to 7-8 inches
BLOOM TIME: summer, fall
SOIL: well-drained, moist, acidic potting soil

Both beautiful and bizarre, this plant has arching flowering stems of flowers and very showy bracts that together are shaped like lobster claws or parrot beaks. Some remind gardeners of bird-of-paradise (*Strelitzia*).

The flowers make about the most interesting cut flowers ever grown. To extend a cut flower's bloom life, cut off the bottom half-inch of stem and submerge the entire flower stalk, leaves, bracts, and all, in room-temperature water for an hour or so. Cut faded flowering stems off near the soil level to make room for more new growth.

Plants usually form large, thick clumps, with large leaves; yellowish leaves are often the result of planting in alkaline soils. Many heliconias are root hardy along the Gulf Coast and in southern California, but are best treated as tender potted plants to be brought indoors in the winter. For best performance, keep yours watered and fertilized during warm months, then reduce water and fertilizer in the cool months of fall. Few pests bother this tropical "ditch weed."

GOOD CHOICES: 'Golden Torch' and 'Lady Di'.

Hibiscus, Chinese
Hibiscus rosa-sinensis
MATURE HEIGHT × WIDTH: 4-7 feet × 3-5 feet
FLOWER COLORS: many plus variegated
FLOWER SIZE: 3-5 inches
BLOOM TIME: all year during warm weather
SOIL: well-drained, moist potting soil

One of the standard tropical plants for large pots, this deep green or variegated but glossy-leaf species will tolerate frost but not freezes. Its splashy single or double blossoms, smooth or ruffled, are large, up to 8 or more inches across. They're available in an astounding array of colors and combinations.

Upright, usually single-trunk specimens have many stems with medium-sized deep green glossy leaves that often turn bright yellow before shedding, causing unnecessary worry for gardeners. They are notorious for shedding most or all of their leaves when brought indoors for overwinter protection; avoid this by pruning plants just as you bring them in the fall, and again just before setting them back out in the spring.

Pinching stem tips helps keep your plants blooming. Whiteflies can be a problem, but not serious; treat with insecticidal soap sprayed on the undersides of leaves where the insects lurk.

GOOD CHOICES: The most consistently popular include 'Fiesta'; 'Kona'; and 'Full Moon'.

Jungle Flame
Ixora coccinea

MATURE HEIGHT × WIDTH: 3-5 feet × 2-3 feet
FLOWER COLORS: red, orange, pink, or yellow
FLOWER SIZE: 1-2 inches
BLOOM TIME: throughout warm weather
SOIL: well-drained, acidic potting soil

Commonly grown outdoors in the hottest parts of our country, ixora has long been a favorite greenhouse flowering plant. It can tolerate all-day sun and heat from spring to fall outdoors in most of the country, or prosper in bright, sunny windows. It must have full light to flower its best, and warm temperatures help as well.

Leaves are 2 to 4 inches long, and produced in whorls. In alkaline soils, the leaves tend to get chlorotic (pale green or yellow with deeper green veins). As with other tropical plants, container-grown ixora is typically smaller and less dense than those grown outdoors in all-year hot weather. Regular tip pruning can help plant density and encourage more flower production.

Unfortunately, ixora is subject to mealybugs, spider mites, and white flies. But regular pruning, feeding, and watering usually keeps the plants putting on new foliage that is not as heavily infested. Or use an insecticidal soap spray.

GOOD CHOICES: 'Orange Sherbet'; 'Pink Pixie'; Malay ixora (*I. duffii*); and 'Super King'.

Mexican Petunia
Ruellia brittoniana

MATURE HEIGHT × WIDTH: 2-5 feet × 2-3 feet
FLOWER COLORS: deep purple, pink, white
FLOWER SIZE: 2- to 3-inch trumpets
BLOOM TIME: spring, summer, fall
SOIL: any potting soil, moist or dry

A "must have" potted perennial from Mexico, this old-fashioned "pass-along" plant is upright but sprawling, with many stems clothed in long, narrow, very dark-green leaves and topped almost continuously with small but still-showy petunialike trumpet flowers.

Though it makes a stunning mass in a large pot all by itself (with pruning to tame its floppy nature), it combines perfectly with other, bolder-textured tropicals where its stems and flowers can weave throughout and provide a bold filler. The dwarf form can be used as a groundcover in larger pots of taller tropical plants. Mexican petunia simply flowers nonstop; a particularly nice habit is how, unlike some plants, it neatly sheds faded flowers into a carpet under the plant.

Easy to prune, easy to root in water or moist soil, the plant is almost weedy, sometimes trying to escape its container through drainage holes. And yet this is one easy plant to grow, and to share.

GOOD CHOICES: 'Purple Showers' is a sterile (noninvasive) variety; 'Chi Chi'; 'Strawberries and Cream'; and 'Katie'.

Orchids
Cattleya, Dendrobium, Phalenopsis, others
MATURE HEIGHT × WIDTH: 9-48 inches × 4-12 inches
FLOWER COLORS: all, and then some
FLOWER SIZE: 1/2-6 inches
BLOOM TIME: all year
SOIL: bark alone, or a super well-drained potting soil

With more than 17,000 species of orchids, perhaps the largest family in the plant kingdom, there naturally has to be at least one that any gardener can grow. Nearly all orchids are grown in pots of very well-drained potting soil, although a good number of "epiphytes" (air plants) are grown in small hanging baskets filled with bark, or wired onto "rafts" of wood.

Getting started with orchids is easy. Just buy a few, put them in a bright window, and keep them humid (out of drafts), moist (not wet), and lightly fed with half-strength or less liquid plant food. Using commercially available orchid soils and fertilizers takes away a lot of guesswork.

GOOD CHOICES: There are too many species and cultivars to list, but here are the most durable kinds. *Cattleya,* with large "corsage" flowers; *Dendrobium* need some direct sunshine; *Phalaenopsis,* the "moth" orchid; *Cymbidium* are terrestrial with long, narrow, grasslike leaves and long-lasting flowers; and *Oncidium* include a wide range of terrestrial orchids.

Princess Flower
Tibouchina urvilleana
MATURE HEIGHT × WIDTH: 5-8 feet × 3-5 feet
FLOWER COLORS: brilliant royal purple
FLOWER SIZE: 3-6 inches wide
BLOOM TIME: spring, summer, fall
SOIL: any well-drained potting soil that is kept moist

This tall, wide, small tree is about the closest you can come to having a glorious tropical tree in a container. Its combination of colors—both the huge flowers and the large leaves—makes the plant worth the trouble it takes to keep it tidy.

New growth and flower buds are covered with velvety orange or red hairs, and the 6-inch, pointed-oval, deeply veined leaves, which are sometimes edged in red, often develop bright red-orange or yellow spots before being shed.

Brilliant, showy flowers, each up to 4 or more inches across and with five velvety royal purple petals, are produced constantly throughout the warm season and indoors in the winter, if kept in a sunny south window away from drafts.

Normally a woody shrub or small tree in its native Brazil, the leggy, somewhat brittle plant needs heavy pruning in the spring and light pruning after each flowering, or it will get ungainly and possibly break indoors.

GOOD CHOICES: 'Athens Blue' (*T. semidecandra*).

Sago
Cycas revoluta
MATURE HEIGHT × WIDTH: 2-4 feet × 2-4 feet
FLOWER COLORS: n/a
FLOWER SIZE: n/a
BLOOM TIME: n/a
SOIL: sandy soils that seldom stay wet

Prehistoric sago palms, which are not true palms, are more closely related to ancient cone-bearing conifers, and were around when dinosaurs roamed the earth. These very popular potted plants are perfect for accents, or as an underplanting for other tropicals. Deep green, glossy foliage is produced all at once in a whorled fountain around a center "cone" that is either male or female; the orange, egg-shaped fruits are very attractive.

Though slow growing, sagos usually sprout lots of small "pups" or small plants around their base. These can be twisted off and replanted in smaller pots; just be careful of the spines hidden deep in their foliage. If the leaves start looking ratty, simply cut them off and enjoy the short, thick trunk that gradually forms. Scale insects are a problem, but can be pruned off with the older leaves.

GOOD CHOICES: The species is the most widely available, except for collectors in the south. Queen sago (*C. circinalis*) is much larger and more dramatic, but is often too large for wintering indoors.

Shell Ginger, Variegated
Alpinia zerumbet
MATURE HEIGHT × WIDTH: 4-5 feet × 3-4 feet
FLOWER COLORS: white or pinkish white
FLOWER SIZE: 1-2 inches, in hanging clusters
BLOOM TIME: spring, summer, fall
SOIL: well-drained potting soil rich in organic matter

Several members of the ginger family are grown as container plants—most with edible, though zesty or hot, tubers used in Oriental cooking. The clump-forming plants (which are easy to divide) generally grow in clumps half or nearly as wide as they are tall. But the variegated shell ginger, with its stunning, lance-shaped foliage, is the grandest of all; mature plants often have foliage with maroon leafstalks. Its sensational flowers are shell-shaped and fragrant.

The bright, lance-shaped leaves really shine when several clumps of this bright ginger are interplanted with large, coarse-textured plants such as schefflera or rubber tree, or large split-leaf philodendrons. They also look great against dark walls in shaded gardens, and when brought indoors for the winter can be grown near (but not directly in) a sunny window.

Cut stalks down when they fade and encourage new growth with regular soakings and light fertilization.

GOOD CHOICES: 'Variegata' and variegated ginger (*A. vittata*).

Other tropicals to try in containers:

- **Bird's Nest Anthurium,** *Anthurium hooken* (top left)

- **Brazilian Plume,** *Justicia carnea*

- **Compact Philodendron,** *Philodendron* × *'Xanadu'*

- **Dumb Cane,** *Dieffenbachia* cultivars (top right)

- **Kumquat,** *Fortunella,* and other compact citrus trees

- **Mother of Thousands, Maternity Plant,** *Kalanchoe daigremontiana*

- **Shrimp Plant,** *Beleperone guttata* (center)

- **Thyrallis,** *Galphimia glauca*

Vines and Climbers

Why would anyone want to grow a vine or climber in a container? In certain cases, it makes good sense. In a small space where gardening area is limited—a balcony, say, or a deck or terrace—vertical-growing plants are an important addition. They make the space more lush, more beautiful and, ultimately, more self-contained and intimate. And some vines are too tender to keep in the ground where one good winter would finish them off; if they are pot-grown, they can be moved safely indoors during the cold weather. There's even a small but significant practical reason. No plant, including a vine, appreciates growing in compacted soil, which happens in busy outdoor spaces where there is foot traffic. A pot-grown vine is safe from this problem, happily enjoying excellent growing soil undisturbed.

But it is not always easy to raise a vine or climber in a pot. You need to give the root system sufficient space (downward as well as to the sides) by selecting a large-enough container. And to grow robustly, producing plentiful foliage and abundant flowers, that root system may be greedy for food and water to support the show overhead. So you, the gardener, have to monitor the situation often and have a generous hand with the hose and fertilizer.

That said, there are certainly worthy vines that prosper in a pot. Here are a few that you can't miss with.

Black-eyed Susan Vine
Thunbergia alata

MATURE HEIGHT: 8 feet
FLOWER COLORS: orange, yellow, white
FLOWER SIZE: 1-1¹/₂ inches
BLOOM TIME: summer
SOIL: well-drained potting soil
ZONES: 9-10; elsewhere, treat like an annual

This is a pretty spectacular plant, sometimes given to rampant growth in the garden proper but easy to manage in a pot. Situate it below a good support such as a trellis or, if practical, plunge that trellis into the pot. (Do this on planting day; once the plant is up and growing, adding a support could become tricky and add the risk of stabbing into the root system.) Medium-green leaves, abetted by twining stems, will then mount the support and, with some tinkering by you, fill it out.

The bright flowers resemble the popular black-eyed Susan, in the sense that they have golden petals and dark centers; they are not actually daisies, but are broadly flaring trumpets. And they are fabulous.

Other ways to show off this vine include in a pot and cascading over the stump of a tree, in a hanging basket, or over a deck railing. It does best with plenty of sunshine.

GOOD CHOICES: 'Alba' is the white version; 'Suzie' has orange-yellow flowers.

Ivy
Hedera helix cultivars

MATURE HEIGHT: varies, can reach 15 feet
FLOWER COLORS: n/a
FLOWER SIZE: n/a
BLOOM TIME: n/a
SOIL: well-drained potting soil
ZONES: 5-10

Taken for granted or even maligned as a weedy groundcover, ivy turns out to be a fine climber for pot culture. The pot keeps it in bounds and allows you to control the growth. Ivy climbs by means of aerial roots, clinging with great determination. Trim back as needed; on the other hand, a thickly grown one can turn out to be a good privacy screen, or to cover an eyesore.

Ivy is also shade-tolerant, which is nice when you want some coverage in otherwise difficult-to-decorate corners. In season, it ought to be watered regularly; if the leaves go limp and papery, you've waited too long.

Try a variegated-leaf cultivar to make an unexpected splash. Or keep everything in scale with a smaller pot and a smaller-leaves cultivar, and enjoy an almost-delicate show. Or invest in a topiary frame, insert it in a big-enough pot, and plant one or more ivy plants all around it until you are showing off a green goose or elephant on your patio!

GOOD CHOICES: 'Gold Heart' and 'Irish Lace'. And there are literally scores more.

Mandevilla

Mandevilla splendens, M. × amabilis

MATURE HEIGHT: 5-10 feet
FLOWER COLORS: pink
FLOWER SIZE: 2-3 inches
BLOOM TIME: summer
SOIL: well-drained, enriched potting soil
ZONES: 10-11

Hailing from southeastern Brazil, this twining beauty is excellent in a pot. The flexible stems bear shiny, ribbed, evergreen leaves that can be up to 5 inches or so broad. The stems have no special way of clinging to their support, so add a trellis, or run a string or wire up where you want it to go.

It likes a sunny window or a sheltered, bright spot outdoors in the summer months. To grow well and produce flower buds, and sustain the flowers, mandevilla really should start out with an enriched growing medium and then be fertilized every few weeks during the growing season.

The flowers are worth the wait! They have a flared trumpet shape, are pink to bright pink with a golden yellow throat, and appear in profusion. Even a plant in a very small pot will bloom. If it is outside, hummingbirds may stop by. In any event, mandevilla is not cold hardy and should be considered an annual or brought indoors in the fall.

GOOD CHOICES: The prettiest pink flower is a cultivar called 'Alice du Pont'.

Moonflower

Ipomoea alba

MATURE HEIGHT: 8-15 feet
FLOWER COLORS: white
FLOWER SIZE: 5-6 inches
BLOOM TIME: summer
SOIL: well-drained potting soil
ZONES: all; fast-growing annual

Imagine coming home in the evening to relax and watch these morning-glory relatives unfurl their big, glowing, satiny white blossoms. As a bonus, the flowers also radiate a rich, haunting perfume. And the show continues all summer long! This is a good one to situate right under a kitchen window so you can savor it from indoors at times.

Luckily, this breathtaking climber is quite easy to grow. If you live in a cold climate, it's wise to start seeds indoors early (nick or soak the seeds to speed germination, or do both) and transplant the seedlings into a big pot later. If you live in a mild climate, just sow the seeds right in the container, and remember to install a support at that time. Even a short string attached at one end to an adjacent stake and the other end tied to the trellis, fence, or porch will work. The plant will grow quickly, covering itself with large, heart-shaped leaves and before long, those incredible flowers.

GOOD CHOICES: 'Giant White' lives up to its name with 6-inch blooms.

Morning Glory
Ipomoea purpurea

MATURE HEIGHT: 5-10 feet
FLOWER COLORS: blue, red, white, and bicolors
FLOWER SIZE: 3 inches
BLOOM TIME: summer
SOIL: well-drained potting soil
ZONES: all; fast-growing annual

For quick, temporary, and plentiful summer color, morning glories are hard to beat. These annual vines are simple to grow in a pot and bloom heavily. They get their name from the fact that they unfurl their jaunty blossoms in the morning and close by afternoon except on cloudy days. Though usually seen in blue, you can now find them in a whole array of wonderful colors.

Sow the seeds early, right in the pot in which they are to mature. Because they germinate slowly, soak them in warm water or nick or scrape the hard coat before planting, just to get them going a little faster.

Do not neglect watering and fertilizing. For training the vines, a string or wire is certainly sufficient, although a lightweight trellis will also do the job. One caveat: The stems are not strong enough to withstand high winds or people brushing past them, so site your potted morning glories in a sheltered spot.

GOOD CHOICES: The classic 'Heavenly Blue'; 'Scarlett O'Hara'; 'Milky Way'; and the Sunrise mix.

Passionflower
Passiflora caerulea

MATURE HEIGHT: 5-10 feet
FLOWER COLORS: purple, blue, pink, white with purple
FLOWER SIZE: 4 inches
BLOOM TIME: summer
SOIL: well-drained potting soil
ZONES: 7-10

A vigorous semitropical vine with remarkable flowers, passion flower grows just fine in a container. In mild climates, it can stay outside year-round; everyone else should bring the pot indoors when cold weather comes.

The complex flowers splay open to show off delicate outer petals, colorful filaments, and prominent center stamens, all in a multitude of colors. Spanish missionaries to the New World bestowed the common name we use today, citing symbolism in the flower parts to signify Christ's passion, including the crown of thorns, hammer, and nails used in the crucifixion, and 10 "petals" for 10 apostles.

Passion flower produces loads of flowers all summer long, holding on with twining tendrils. Keep the pot evenly moist, but don't overwater or the roots may suffer. By autumn, the flowers yield to a crop of small, yellow-orange, egg-shaped fruits, which, while not harmful, don't have much flavor. Still, they prolong the vine's season of interest.

GOOD CHOICES: 'Constance Elliott' has fragrant white blooms; 'Grandiflora' has bigger, 6-inch flowers.

Sweet Pea
Lathyrus odoratus
MATURE HEIGHT: 4-6 feet
FLOWER COLORS: purples, pinks white, bicolors
FLOWER SIZE: 1¹/₂-2 inches
BLOOM TIME: late spring to summer
SOIL: well-drained, enriched potting soil
ZONES: all; fast-growing annual

Container gardeners need not be denied the pleasure of growing colorful, sweetly perfumed sweet peas. The main things to remember are water and temperature.

Sweet peas do not like it hot. So start them in spring and choose a spot for them that isn't in blazing hot sun. The side of a patio or deck is good, perhaps where you can train their growth up a line of string.

Sow seeds ahead of time indoors and move them into larger pots outside as soon as all danger of frost is past. They have a hard seed coat, so soak seeds overnight and perhaps nick them with a knife to nudge them along.

The plants attach to supports with grasping tendrils, which appear quickly, so you need to install that support or guiding string when you bring them to their chosen spot. For more better-quality flowers, fertilize and water regularly and deeply. Pinch out tops to encourage strong side growth.

GOOD CHOICES: The 'Mammoth Early' strain; and 'Old Spice'.

Sweet Potato Vine
Ipomoea batatas
MATURE HEIGHT: 8-15 feet
FLOWER COLORS: lavender
FLOWER SIZE: 1-inch trumpets
BLOOM TIME: summer
SOIL: well-drained, rich potting soil
ZONES: 9-11; grown as an ornamental annual

On the lookout for an unusual but easy vine? Sweet potato vine—yes, the same plant that makes those tasty orange-fleshed tubers—fills the bill. But as a potted plant enjoyed for its ornamental foliage, it's much less demanding.

Grow it in a well-drained but organically rich soil mix. Small plants are available from garden centers and, in recent years, interesting leaf colors have been the big draw; there's a chartreuse-leaved one and another with foliage so dark it's almost black. The leaf shapes are also intriguing, sometimes heart-shaped, sometimes with deep lobes.

Sweet potato vine is a wonderful supporting player in pots and hanging baskets. It grows lushly, spilling over the sides, and its colors can contrast or complement whatever you choose to combine it with. It endures summer heat and tolerates shade. With regular water and occasional clipping back of errant stems, it will go like gangbusters all summer, succumbing at last when cold weather arrives.

GOOD CHOICES: 'Blackie'; 'Marguerite'; and the recent introduction Tricolor' ('Pink Frost').

Other vines and climbers to try in containers:

- **Cup-and-Saucer Vine,** Cobaea scandens
- **Gourds,** Lagenaria siceraria (top left)
- **Hardy Kiwi,** Actinidia kolomikta (top right)
- **Hops,** Humulus lupulus cultivars

- **Nasturtium, trailing varieties,** Tropaeolum majus
- **Scarlet Runner Bean,** Phaseolus coccineus (center)
- **Vinca, trailing,** Vinca major 'Variegata' and V. minor

photography credits

Felder Rushing: 3, 5, 8A, 8B, 9, 10, 12, 15, 16, 19B, 20, 21A, 21B, 22, 23B, 24, 25B, 29, 30A, 30B, 32, 34, 35, 36, 40, 42, 43, 44, 52, 53, 55, 56, 57, 58, 59, 60A, 60B, 61A, 61B, 62A, 62B, 63, 64A, 64B, 64C, 65, 66A, 66B, 67A, 67B, 68A, 68B, 68C, 69A, 69B, 70A, 70B, 71A, 71B, 72A, 72B, 73, 74A, 74B, 75A, 75B, 75C, 76A, 76B, 76C, 77A, 77B, 78B, 79A, 80A, 80B, 81A, 81B, 82, 85, 92B, 105A, 106A, 106B, 108A, 109A, 109B, 109C, 111A, 119B, 121B, 123A, 125B, 126A, 126B, 127B, 128A, 128B, 129A, 147B, 149A, 149B, 150A, 155B, 156A, 156B, 157B, 160B, 163C, 175 (photo courtesy of the author)

Thomas Eltzroth: 87A, 88A, 89A, 89B, 90A, 92A, 93A, 93B, 94A, 94B, 95A, 96, 97A, 98A, 99B, 100B, 102A, 103A, 103C, 107A, 107B, 110, 111B, 112A, 113A, 113B, 114A, 114B, 115A, 116A, 116B, 117A, 118A, 118B, 119A, 119C, 120, 122A, 123B, 124A, 124B, 125A, 127A, 131A, 131B, 132A, 132B, 133A, 133B, 134A, 135A, 135B, 138A, 139A, 139C, 141A, 142A, 142B, 143A, 144B, 145B, 148A, 148B, 152A, 153B, 154A, 155A, 157A, 157C, 159A, 160A, 161A, 161B, 162B, 163A

Jerry Pavia: 14, 18, 25A, 27, 28, 38, 45, 47, 48, 49, 54, 70C, 78A, 79B, 84, 86, 87B, 90B, 91A, 91B, 95C, 102B, 104, 105B, 129B, 136A, 136B, 137A, 139B, 141B, 144A, 145C, 151A, 154B, 159B

Liz Ball and Rick Ray: 95B, 97B, 98B, 100A, 101A, 101B, 103B, 112B, 115B, 130, 140, 145A, 147A, 162A

Charles Mann: 5, 6, 7, 11, 13, 17, 19A, 23A, 46, 51A, 51B, 83, 99A, 158

William Adams: 146, 150A, 151B, 153A

Lorenzo Gunn: 121A, 129C, 143B

Pamela Harper: 134B, 152B

Dr. Mike Dirr: 163B

Peter Loewer: 39

Mulberry Creek Herb Farm (www.mulberrycreek.com): 117B

Mark Turner: 137B

index

garden notes

garden notes

meet the authors

Felder Rushing

Felder Rushing is a 10th-generation American gardener, whose cluttered but celebrated cottage garden in Jackson, Mississippi, is shared with his wife and best friend Terryl and their teenage children. He has had hundreds of articles and photographs published in dozens of magazines including *Horticulture, Better Homes and Gardens, Fine Gardening, National Geographic, Southern Living, Organic Gardening, Landscape Architecture,* and *Garden Design,* and he has written or co-authored more than a dozen gardening books. He hosts a syndicated public radio garden program, and has taken his TV crew to document European cottage gardens. The American Horticulture Society board member, who has given hundreds of light-hearted gardening lectures coast to coast and across four continents, spends much of his spare time watering his many dozens of potted plants.

Teri Dunn

Teri Dunn is a freelance writer and editor. She is a former Senior Copy Writer for Jackson & Perkins. Her articles on roses, perennials, herbs, waterlilies, wildflowers, and other topics have appeared in *Horticulture Magazine,* for which she worked for many years as an Associate Editor. Teri is the author of numerous other gardening titles, including *Beautiful Roses Made Easy; Selecting, Growing, and Combining Outstanding Perennials; Potting Places: Creative Ideas for Practical Gardening Workplaces; Cottage Gardens; 600 Essential Plants;* and several books in the popular 100 Favorites series on roses, perennials, herbs, shade plants, and others. She resides on Cape Ann, Massachusetts, with her husband Shawn and sons Wes and Tristan.